POCKET GUIDE
TO
DETROIT & MICHIGAN
RESTAURANTS

(including Windsor & Sarnia, Ontario)

Sandra Silfven

MOMENTUM BOOKS LTD.

To Pete

Manufactured in the United States of America

Cover design by Don Ross

Momentum Books Ltd.
Business Office:
2051 Warrington Road
Rochester Hills, MI 48063

ISBN 0-9618726-2-4 Standard Edition
ISBN 0-9618726-3-2 Deluxe Edition

Pocket Guide
to
Detroit & Michigan
Restaurants

CONTENTS

A WORD FROM THE PUBLISHER

The easiest part of publishing this book was the selection of Sandra Silfven to write it.

Our goal was to create the finest pocket restaurant guide, not just for Detroit and Michigan and neighboring Ontario, but the finest ever published anywhere. So we went after the pro who has best demonstrated knowledge of the field, objectivity, integrity, and outstanding writing talent. As Silfven proves on every page, we found what we were looking for.

Silfven's scouting reports on the tables of Michigan have appeared in the pages of *The Detroit News* since the late fall of 1981. And before that, as *The News'* food editor, she shared with readers how restaurant dishes were prepared, even divulging the recipe for a decent copy of deep-dish pizza, Detroit style.

Trust her. She doesn't judge restaurants cavalierly. Spend one meal with Silfven and you'll see she doesn't give credit unless it is due. She appreciates good cooking, good service, unspotted silver, clean restrooms, and tidy parking lots. She knows value when she sees it. And the ratings reflect this.

I've eaten lots of meals in lots of places — including many of those covered in these pages — and in a lot of spots that will never pass muster with Silfven. When it comes to eating out, there is no one — anywhere — whose judgment I trust more than Sandra Silfven. Your palate and your pocketbook are in good hands.

Bill Haney

A WORD FROM THE AUTHOR

Vital information is what diners need. That's true whether they're in a last-minute rush or planning an evening two weeks ahead. So that's what I've tried to deliver in this first-ever comprehensive guide to the restaurants of the Detroit area, Windsor, Ann Arbor, Traverse City—and even Union Pier if you're out that way. Or if you happen to be near Grand Rapids, Kalamazoo, Port Huron, or Clare—anywhere in outstate or upstate or downstate or across the border in Ontario—you'll find plain but wholesome fare and stylish dining, too.

Looking for a quiet spot? Maybe something ethnic? Maybe offbeat? Let's see: How much will it cost? What is the nearest cross street? What is the specialty? And how does it rate?

White tablecloth, no tablecloth—there are restaurants listed here where you sit on the floor. The diversity of restaurants in Metro Detroit—and the entire state—is astonishing.

These pages will unfold for you, in alphabetical order and user-friendly indexes, the wonderful dining experiences Michigan has to offer. Everything from Leo Derderian's "earthy" Anchor Bar to the starched linens of the Golden Mushroom. Everything from burgers to foie gras.

With this handy guide, all you have to do is check the multi-faceted index section to find a family restaurant in West Bloomfield or an upscale spot in Petoskey. You can zero in on places to stop after the theatre, find a romantic setting, or choose a place for the family or the gang. It's all in the indexes—every cuisine, every dining feature under the sun. (Well, almost.) Take a minute to read the Contents page to see the surprises we've served up for you in those indexes.

The actual descriptions are brief—you don't have time to read at length about the sunlight dancing off the rims of crystal glasses.

Basically, each restaurant description gives you a feel for the place—the kind of food, the kind of ambiance, maybe the kind of people who go there. Simple abbreviations explain which meals are served, and dollar signs indicate the cost.

Whenever possible, the restaurants are rated, a job not taken lightly. Stars (☆) indicate my opinion of the place, with five being the highest. You will notice there are not many five star restaurants, nor are the chosen

few found only among the white tablecloth sort —
there is indeed such a thing as a five star corned beef
sandwich.

If an establishment fully delivers what it appears to
promise, it gets a top rating. The total experience —
food, service, and atmosphere — is what matters.

If there are no stars, then the place is (1) brand new
and hasn't been visited; (2) is an established restaurant
that for one reason or another has not yet been scruti-
nized by the critic's eye; or (3) is in a state of transition
to a new cuisine, style, ambiance, or location. (But if
you need those stars, wait until we issue the 1991 edition of this book — they'll be there.)

If you think I've missed something, if you have
thoughts you want to share, or if you want to be sure
of getting your copies of next year's edition hot off the
press for yourself and friends, there is a mailing form
for that in the back of this book. And, oh yes, there's a
form you might want to use for making your own
personal favorites list — or hit list.

My very astute (and hungry) publisher, Bill Haney,
who loves offbeat eateries, molded all this work into
book form. A computer whiz and research fanatic
named Natasha Monchak made sure all the right computer codes were entered and the facts were straight.
(She's a restaurant junkie, too — that helps.) Besides
restaurant addictions, the three of us have at least one
other thing in common — we hope this Guide will be
your companion and road map to the notable restaurants of Michigan.

Sandra Silfven

HOW TO USE THIS GUIDE

THE RATINGS

First of all, remember that every restaurant in this Guide has merit or we wouldn't include it. We kept symbols and abbreviations to a minimum. The star system, an elaboration of the one used in *The Detroit News*, is employed here. This is how it works:

☆	Good (At least some redeeming features.)
☆ ☆	Very Good (This place is cooking!)
☆ ☆ ☆	Excellent (Now, I'm serious. Get a baby-sitter. This spot is hot.)
☆ ☆ ☆ ☆	Outstanding (Cancel everything and go! Whether humble or haute, it delivers what it promises.)
☆ ☆ ☆ ☆ ☆	Superb (Nobody does it better.)
NO STARS	Recommended but not rated yet.

SYMBOLS AND ABBREVIATIONS

Besides the rating, the only abbreviations are dollar signs and letters like B,L,D. Those, of course, stand for breakfast, lunch, and dinner. The dollar signs cue you to the cost of a dinner. Phone numbers are for area code 313, unless specified otherwise.

Since it is almost impossible to estimate how much your personal dinner will cost — everybody has a different appetite — these dollar signs simply represent the average cost of a dinner entree, a good indication of the cost of the entire meal.

Here's the translation:

$	inexpensive (most entrees are less than $7)
$$	moderate (most entrees are from $7 to $13)
$$$	expensive (most entrees are from $13 to $19)
$$$$	very expensive (most entrees are $19 or more)

INDEXES

There will be times when you don't want to just thumb through an alphabetical list and hope you get lucky. You may care only about one specific characteristic — location or type of cuisine, or a special quality or feature. Okay, that's what the indexes are for. Simply flip to the back for a breakdown of the restaurants according to location, cuisine, and curious things such as the view and whether or not it's romantic, a power scene, or whatever. You just want a spot with some peace and quiet? There's a listing for that.

Even if you're looking for a spot to hold your class reunion, need a caterer, or wonder how much to tip, we have suggestions.

To help you find your way to the restaurants included in this Guide, we have provided a map and a listing showing the pertinent cities, townships, and counties located within each region.

S.S.

ALPHABETICAL
DIRECTORY OF
RESTAURANTS

Ah Wok
in Novi Plaza, 41563 W. 10 Mile, Novi. 349-9260.
L,D. $$
Respected Chinese eatery deserves gourmet reputation. Loyal patrons swear by Szechuan shrimp with peapods and water chestnuts, velvet chicken with straw mushrooms, and a steamed whole pickerel with ginger and garlic. Peking duck available with advance notice. Pleasant but unpretentious setting doesn't rest on ethnic cliches.   ☆ ☆ ☆

Akasaka Japanese Restaurant
in Laurel Commons, 37152 Six Mile (at Newburgh), Livonia. 462-2630. L,D. $$
Shades of soft mauve and gray plus miles of light wood complement freshness of sushi and sashimi. Be proficient in chopsticks or be square—clientele is primarily Japanese. Tempura, udon dishes, nabemono.
☆ ☆

Al's Lounge
7940 South (at West End), Detroit. 841-5677.
L,D. $
An anchor of the Hungarian community for 45 years, though little of the original neighborhood remains. Still operated by the family of Al Kazensky. Favorite dishes remain chicken paprikash and stuffed cabbage. Dining room is a time trip back to the '40s.   ☆

Alban's
190 N. Hunter (at Maple), Birmingham. 258-5788.
L,D. $$
Contemporary, bi-level room with signature "Big Wheel" deli sandwich plus salads, whitefish, and steak. A sister business to adjacent Bottle & Basket wine shop, the Cruvinet is well stocked. More than two dozen wines by the glass.   ☆ ☆

Alexander's
4265 Woodward (at Canfield), Detroit. 831-2662.
L,D. $$
Popular jazz club offers pizza, ribs, steak, and salad. Good stop-off after an evening at the nearby Fox Theatre.   ☆

Alibi Lounge
6720 Rochester Rd. (s. of South Blvd.), Troy.
879-0014. L,D. $
A bar where kids are welcome. Dimly lit dining
room is still bright enough to spy the sea of Formica
tables surrounded by parents and children devouring
pizza. Greek salad, burgers, fish & chips, and spaghetti.   ☆

Amadeus Cafe-Patisserie
122 E. Washington (bet. Main & 4th Ave.), Ann
Arbor. 665-8767. L,D. Sun. Brunch. $
An Eastern European cafe that hasn't forgotten its
roots. Ruffled window sheers and Mozart set the
stage for bigos (hearty stew of sauerkraut, cabbage
and kielbasa), pork cutlet prepared in the style of
wiener schnitzel, pierogi, chicken paprikash, and
open-face sandwiches on rye. Tortes are a specialty;
the coffee rum tastes like straight espresso.   ☆ ☆

American and Lafayette Coney Islands
114 and 118 W. Lafayette (at Michigan), Detroit.
961-7758 and 964-8198. B,L,D. $
Downtown Detroit's two legendary coneys, owned
by cousins, have nourished everybody from cops on
the beat to judges at nearby courtrooms. Hot
dogs—lathered in chili, chopped onions, and
mustard—are the kind that sputter and spit juice in
your eye.   ☆

America's Pizza Cafe
24459 Telegraph Rd. (at 10 Mile), Southfield.
352-5588. L,D. $
Little Caesar's Mike Ilitch is trying something new:
individual-sized gourmet pizzas baked in a wood-
fired oven in the center of a full-service art-deco
eatery. Experimental restaurant also offers pastas,
chicken, and desserts. Beer, wine, and espresso. ☆ ☆

Anchor Bar
525 W. Lafayette (at Second), Detroit. 964-9127.
L,D. $
Newspaper and TV reporters call this place home,
but they rarely consume anything more solid than a
burger and a bag of chips. Pictures over the bar are
of notable customers, many of them reporters and
downtown celebrities. They all have one thing in
common: they're dead.   ☆

Andante

321 Bay, Petoskey. (616) 348–3321. D. $$$$
Quaint white frame house with white wicker furniture out front and a great view of the harbor of Little Traverse Bay. Robert Stark's new entry in the up-north upscale market consists of complex presentations such as beef tenderloin with grilled garlic polenta, veal medallions with braised leeks, and sundried tomato fettucine with chanterelle mushroom sauce and sliced pheasant breast.   ☆ ☆ ☆

Andiamo Italia Ristorante

7096 E. 14 Mile (w. of Van Dyke), Warren.
268-3200. L,D. $$
Pretty serious, pretty inexpensive, and just plain pretty. The far east side's newest Italian entry has gnocchi so light they float off the plate. Homemade pastas are powered with garlic and bathed in olive oil. Excellent veal and chicken. And no cliches!
                              ☆ ☆ ☆

Andrew's on the Corner

201 Jos. Campau (at Atwater), Detroit. 259-8325.
L,D. $
Popular meeting spot for young execs from nearby Stroh headquarters, and they don't drink Coors. Typical bar grub plus nice plate of breaded perch and coleslaw.   ☆

Angelo's

1100 E. Catherine (at Glen), Ann Arbor. 761-8996.
B,L. $
Cherished breakfast spot where homemade raisin toast has nourished U-M med students for 30 years. Waffles and pancakes are longtime specialties. Deep-fried homemade French toast smothered with fruit and whipped cream is new. Coffee is brewed from fresh-ground beans; o.j. is fresh-squeezed.   ☆ ☆ ☆

Antler's, The

804 Portage (2 blks. e. of the Power Canal), Sault
Ste. Marie. (906) 632-3571. L,D. $
Fun family tavern with everything from canoes to stuffed snakes adorning ceiling and walls. Whistles and sirens from behind the bar can be heard by passing freighters in the nearby shipping channel. Menu is wild, too: 80 items that range from Paul Bunyan burgers to lobster tails.   ☆

Antonio's

in Kimberly Corner of Shops, 20311 Mack (at Loch-moor), Grosse Pointe Woods. 884-0253. D. $$
One of the better Italian additions to the east side, though garden atmosphere is a bit contrived. Cooking style is reminiscent of Artie Oliverio's, which is not surprising since Artie and Antonio Scerri, the owner, once worked together. Piquant veal and chicken, plus the appetizer everybody orders — scamorza, a layering of bread, mozzarella, and prosciutto in lemon butter.   ☆ ☆ ☆

Appe'teaser II

in the Great American Insurance Building, 280 N. Woodward (at Willits), Birmingham. 646-7001. L,D. $$
Smart, atrium eatery known for interesting American food: broad menu includes coconut shrimp, chicken livers with fresh strawberries, shrimp & scallops with pea pods poached in white wine. Also at 335 N. Main, Milford, 685-0989. Milford eatery is more casual, especially popular with families. ☆ ☆

Arboretum

7075 S. Lake Shore (M-119) (3 mi. n. of Harbor Springs), Harbor Springs. (616) 526-6291. D. $$$
On the cutting edge of gourmet. Claims to fame are the marinated baby lamb racks and lengthy wine list. Forest of ficus trees, Norfolk pines, and rubber trees accounts for the name.

Archers

2395 Woodward (at Square Lake), Bloomfield Hills. 334-4561. L,D. $$$
Deluxe adult restaurant with Manhattan-slick bar and sedate dining room. Owner Chuck Archer used to manage Excalibur. Haute American/Continental cooking: Dover sole, tournedos with peppercorns, escargots in puff pastry.   ☆ ☆ ☆

Arie's Cafe

127 E. Bridge, Plainwell. (616) 685-9495. L,D. $$
Turn-of-century storefront known for gourmet food at family restaurant prices. Sauteed whitefish with lemon, capers, and tomato; grilled leg of lamb; prime rib with barbecue sauce; homemade pasta. For dessert, homemade peanut butter pie, chocolate truffle cake, and fresh fruit with Grand Marnier sauce.

Bagley Cafe
3354 Bagley (bet. 23rd & I-75), Detroit. 842–1880.
D. $$
Intimate, low-key Spanish eatery with light appe-
tizers called tapas—grilled whole shrimp, potatoes
with garlic sauce, and steamed mussels. Entrees
include grilled meats showered with oregano and
thyme, plus cold sliced omelets and a marvelous
prosciutto-stuffed rainbow trout. Specialty is paella.
☆ ☆ ☆

Bangkok Club
in Southfield Commons, 29269 Southfield (n. of 12
Mile), Southfield. 569–1400. L,D. $$
Thai food goes big time in old Restaurant Duglass
digs. Elegant dining room with section of Thai
sunken tables and vividly colored floor cushions is
home to intricate curries, stir-frys, and grilled seafood. The menu is mostly a la carte, but a half
dozen fixed-price dinners take the mystery out of
ordering. ☆ ☆

Bangkok Cuisine
in Meijer Shopping Center, 2240 16 Mile (at Dequin-
dre), Sterling Heights. 977–0130. L,D. $
Extensive Thai menu including crunchy spring rolls,
satay with peanut sauce, curried shrimp, and homemade coconut ice cream. Nondescript exterior is foil
for charm inside. Especially popular at lunch. Also
at 34360 Groesbeck Hwy., Fraser, 790–3710. ☆ ☆ ☆

Bangkok Express
254 W. 9 Mile, Ferndale. 545–8760. L,D. $
The "McDonald's" of Detroit area Thai food. Step
up to the counter, read the menu printed on over-
head board, and help yourself to plastic silverware
and styrofoam. Spicy shrimp with shredded vegetables, bean curd showered with crushed peanuts,
fried rice. ☆

Bavarian Inn
713 S. Main (downtown near the covered bridge),
Frankenmuth. (517) 652–9941. L,D. $$
All-you-can-eat chicken dinner leaves you hollering
for help. Spread also includes three German breads,
chicken noodle soup, four salads, dressing, mashed
potatoes, gravy, egg noodles, vegetable, and ice
cream. ☆ ☆

Bavarian Inn Ratskeller

in the Bavarian Inn, 1280 Ouellette (bet. Tecumseh & Chides), Windsor, Ontario. (519) 254-5123. L,D. $$

Bavarian-born Raimund and Jutta Berberich not only remodeled the motel in German style, but built themselves a homey German restaurant. Bavarian platter for two offers tastes of everything: smoked pork loin, bratwurst, wiener schnitzel, potato croquettes, and sauerkraut. A good tomato-onion salad for starters and special Salzburger Nockeln for dessert — if you arrange for it ahead of time. ☆ ☆

Beau Jack's

4108 W. Maple (w. of Telegraph), Birmingham. 626-2630. L,D. $$

Noshing spot for Bloomfield golfers and Vic Tanny workout fiends. Broad menu offers heart-healthy dishes, famous gourmet burgers, entree salads (Caesar with grilled chicken), sauteed perch and broiled whitefish. More than a dozen wines by the glass.

☆ ☆

Beggar's Banquet

218 Abbott Rd. (off Grand River), E. Lansing. (517) 351-4573. B,L,D. Sun. Brunch. $$

Atmosphere may be casual, but the food is taken seriously. Innovative cooking and lots of daily specials. At breakfast, omelets, eggs Benedict; for lunch, interesting sandwiches and a great big burger; at dinner, chicken Kiev, sauteed whitefish flamed with Frangelico, and London broil. Extensive wine list. ☆ ☆ ☆

Bella Ciao

118 W. Liberty (bet. Main & Ashley), Ann Arbor. 995-2107. D. $$

Small, intimate and Italian. Top-grade veal, salads, and pasta are twirled with everything from chicken livers to sweet red peppers. Vegetarians are welcome; Italian wine lovers will think they're in heaven. Make a reservation or you'll be sorry. ☆ ☆ ☆

Most entrees:		No stars	Not Rated
$	= less than $7	☆	Good
$$	= $7 to $13	☆ ☆	Very Good
$$$	= $13 to $19	☆ ☆ ☆	Excellent
$$$$	= $19 or more	☆ ☆ ☆ ☆	Outstanding
		☆ ☆ ☆ ☆ ☆	Superb
See p. xi for explanations.			

Benno's
1436 Brush (s. of Madison), Detroit. 961-5141. D.
$$$
Some nights, owner Benno Steinborn does it all —
hosts, serves, and cooks. Small, elegant dining room
showcases good taste in antiques. Uncomplicated
European menu of beef Wellington, oven-roasted
potatoes and a fruited egg dessert called Omelet
Stephanie. (At time of printing, Benno's was slated
to move to Royal Oak.)   ☆ ☆

Betty Ross II
28726 John R (at 12 Mile), Madison Heights.
541-1353. B,L,D. $
Mecca of country music and country ham. All-day
Southern breakfast menu provides biscuits and
gravy, assorted style eggs and bacon, plus griddle-
fried corn bread. Yahoo!   ☆

Beverly Hills Grill
31471 Southfield (n. of 13 Mile), Birmingham.
642-2355. B,L,D. Sun. Brunch. $$
Restrained coastal decor and free rein "new Ameri-
can" cooking. Monthly changing menu features
items like roasted garlic with chevre and red peppers, grilled yellow fin tuna on multi-grain bread,
and smoked duck ravioli. Chef Robert Kaslly's surprise feast is breakfast: bowls of dew-fresh berries,
pineapple glazed with brown sugar, huevos ranche-
ros, and homemade corned beef hash topped with
melted cheddar and poached eggs. Consistently
innovative food.   ☆ ☆ ☆ ☆

Bijou
30855 Southfield (at 13 Mile), Southfield. 644-5522.
L,D. $$$$
Cinema ambiance matches drama of owner Walter
Maeder's tableside cooking. Shrimps Pernod, Caesar
salad, and flamed desserts like crepes Suzette.
Entrees are mainstream Continental: salmon with
Hollandaise, filet mignon with Bearnaise, and the
house favorite, roast rack of lamb, Javanese style.
Wine list is heavy in French Burgundies.   ☆ ☆ ☆

Prix fixe refers to a multi-course meal with one flat price.
Sometimes dessert is extra. Drinks and the tip always are.

Better to overdress than underdress. In the Midwest, coat
and tie are preferred dress at better restaurants.

Billie's Boathouse
449 Water St. (at Mary), Saugatuck. (616) 857-1188.
L,D. $$
Hangout for the yachting crowd. Appropriate port-
holes allow glimpses of passing boats in the harbor.
American and Mexican menu. Most people can't
finish the ample wet burrito. "Wild" tostada is
another hot seller, along with perch and prime rib.
Jazz band nightly.

Black Pearl
3955 Woodward, (at Alexandrine), Detroit.
831-0042. L,D. $$
Neighborhood may be neglected, but not Gerri
Allen's soul cooking. Smothered chicken, short ribs,
fried or smothered pork chops, collard greens, can-
died sweet potatoes, and okra. Dinners come with
two side dishes plus cucumber salad and hot-water
corn bread. Fresh-made lemonade and peach cobbler. Nobody walks away hungry.   ☆ ☆

Blaney Inn
M-77 (1 mi. n. of US 2), Blaney Park.
(906) 283-3417. D. $$
Former resort, and before that a logging camp in
the 1920s. Whitefish and steaks. All-you-can-eat
family dinners on Sunday. Open Memorial Day to
early October.

Blue Danube
1235 Ottawa St. E. (1 blk. from Parent), Windsor,
Ontario. (519) 252-0246 (or in Detroit 963-1903).
L,D. $$
Gypsy all the way—music, food, wine, hospitality.
Specialties are Hungarian paprikash, goulash, veal
schnitzel, and ultimate combination plates: the
"Transylvanian Platter" for two and the "Budapest
Platter" for four.   ☆ ☆

Blue Nile, The
in Trapper's Alley, 508 Monroe (bet. Brush & Beau-
bien), Detroit. 964-6699. L,D. $$$
Authentic Ethiopian feasts, but only at dinner.
Guests sit on floor-level carved wood chairs at "bas-
ket" tables. Stewed meats, lentils, split peas, salad,
and spongy bread called injera. At lunch, an Ameri-
can menu: broiled seafood, shrimp primavera, and
chicken.   ☆ ☆ ☆

Blue Pointe
17131 E. Warren (off Cadieux), Detroit. 882–3653.
L,D. Sun. Brunch. $
Atmosphere may not win awards, but the food
delivers. Unadorned broiled seafood (monkfish,
trout, sea scallops, and whitefish), plus smattering
of pasta—homemade gnocchi, lasagna, and ravioli.

☆ ☆

Bluebird Restaurant & Bar
102 River, Leland. (616) 256–9081. L,D. $$
Casual, shirt-sleeve spot on banks of Leland River
broils some of the freshest whitefish up north.
Founded as a sandwich and soda shop by boat
builders Martin and Leone Telgard in 1927, it has
grown to a 180-seat full-service eatery, noted for
seafood and cinnamon rolls. Good selection of
Michigan wines. ☆ ☆

Boone's Long Lake Inn
7208 Secor (off Silver Lake Rd.), Traverse City.
(616) 946–3991. D. $$
Talk about bargains: Barry Boone's 18-ounce steak
for $10.95 may be the talk of Traverse City, but
other specialties raise eyebrows, too. Wednesday is
shrimp night—all you can eat for $12.95. Sunday is
prime rib—a 12-ounce cut for $8.95 or 22 ounces
for $10.95. Home-baked bread, cole slaw, and
potato included.

Botsford Inn, The
28000 Grand River (at 8 Mile), Farmington Hills.
474–4800. B,L,D. Sun. Brunch. $$$
Historic stagecoach stop, at one time owned by
Henry Ford. Rooms still boast many old Ford pos-
sessions. Homey, old-style menu: chicken pot pie,
fresh roasted turkey, braised short ribs, and fresh
baked pies. ☆ ☆

Bouquets
in Radisson Plaza Hotel, 1500 Town Center (10 1/2
& Evergreen), Southfield. 827–4143. L,D. $$$
Kudos to nouvelle plate presentations, exceptional
fresh-ground coffee, homemade ice creams, and
zealous wine list. Tequila-flamed shrimp in citrus
butter sauce complement Villeroy & Boch table
service and thin stemware. Fresh fish daily, plus
New York strip. ☆ ☆ ☆

Bower's Harbor Inn

on the Old Mission Peninsula, 13512 Peninsula Dr.
(9 mi. out the peninsula), Traverse City.
(616) 223-4222. D. $$$
Lovely old home overlooking Grand Traverse Bay
draws regular customers such as Gov. Blanchard for
"fish in a bag," pecan-dredged walleye, and gar-
licked filet of beef. Country breakfast buffet on
Sunday. Bowery Restaurant behind the inn is more
casual.   ☆ ☆

Bravo!

5402 Portage (bet. Kilgore & Milham), Kalamazoo.
(616) 344-7700. L,D. Sun. Brunch. $$$
It's the white butcher paper and crayon scenario in
this new Italian-American eatery. Saltimbocca alla
Romano, veal with porcini mushrooms, grilled yellow fin tuna with tomato and basil. "Cafe" section
offers lighter sandwiches, pizza, entree salads, and
pastas.

Bread Basket Deli, The

in Lincoln Center, 26052 Greenfield (n. of 10 Mile),
Oak Park. 968-0022. B,L,D. $
One of the area's best delis, if not THE best for
juicy two-fisted corned beef sandwiches thick as
telephone directories and matzoh balls so huge they
make the chicken soup look silly. Atmosphere is
pandemonium.   ☆ ☆ ☆ ☆

Brewery, The

39950 Hayes (n. of 17 Mile), Mt. Clemens.
286-3020. L,D. $$
Scotch, filet mignon, and businessmen stretching
their lunch hour. Popular Macomb Cty. haunt has
enormous bar and cozy dining rooms. Good ribs,
long list of seafood. Extremely clean. Same owners
operate Mr. Paul's Chop House, also in Mt.
Clemens.   ☆ ☆

Bridges Restaurant

in the Holiday Inn, 1498 Venetian Blvd. (off 402,
Marina Rd. exit), Sarnia, Ontario. (519) 336-6100.
B,L,D. Sun. Brunch. $$$
Dining room overlooks river and golf course. Steak,
prime rib, seafood. Lunch buffet daily (except Saturday); also Sunday brunch. The 6:30 a.m. breakfast is one of the earliest in town.

Brigantino
851 Erie St. E. (at Ellesmere), Windsor, Ontario.
(519) 254-7041. L,D. $$
Flame-red linens and flowers poking out of chianti
bottles may be predictable, but delicious jumbo
mussels ribboned with high-voltage tomato and
garlic are a surprise. Excellent garlic bread crowned
with a thin slice of fresh tomato and powdering of
Parmesan, plus stylish antipasto of meats, cheeses,
and never enough olives. Lasagna is four-stories
high.   ☆ ☆ ☆

Britts' Cafe at Silver's
151 W. Fort (at Shelby), Detroit. 963-4866. B,L. $
A health-conscious cafeteria with eclectic specials
such as mixed vegetable phyllo triangles, and jumbo
pasta shells stuffed with chicken. Always a fresh
fruit compote, romaine salad with croutons, deli
sandwiches, and jumbo muffins. Continental break-
fast beginning at 8:30 a.m. Jim Britt is "committed
to reducing my customers' fat intake."   ☆ ☆ ☆

Brothers Bar-b-que
18091 Wyoming, (at Curtis), Detroit. 864-2634.
L,D. $$
Famous for the "boogaloo" sandwich—a sinful stack
of cheese, ground pork, barbecue sauce, and onions
on a French bun. Barbecued ribs, chicken, and fried
shrimp.   ☆

Bubi's Awesome Eats
620 University W. (at Jeanette) Windsor, Ontario.
(519) 252-2001. L,D. $
Zany spot where hottest item is cold: frozen yogurt
called "frogurt." A noisy machine mashes frogurt
with the flavoring of your choice (everything from
fresh fruit to hard candies). You won't believe the
black ball and sour cherry combo, or the water-
melon. The owner calculated there were 5,461,512
non-repetitive flavor combinations. More substantial
eats include burgers in nearly as many weird varia-
tions, plus lots of salads, a few sandwiches, and
cheesecake.   ☆ ☆

A Cruvinet is a storage system for preserving opened bottles of wine. This service allows a customer the opportu-
nity to order just one glass of something rare or special.
Some of the most interesting wines "on tap" are at Opus
One in Detroit.

Buddy's Pizza
31646 Northwestern Hwy., (just w. of Middlebelt),
Farmington Hills. 855-4600. L,D. $$
A Detroit favorite: thick, square pizza—ribboned
with sauce, heaped with pepperoni and onions, bur-
ied under cheese. So good you want to cry. Soups,
pastas, burgers, and a nice Greek salad, too. Arrive
early or prepare to wait for a table. Other locations:
original Buddy's, 17125 Conant (at 6 Mile), Detroit,
892-9001; plus eateries at 33605 Plymouth (bet.
Farmington & Stark Rds.), Livonia, 261-3550; 4370
Highland Rd. (e. of Pontiac Lake Rd.), Waterford,
683-3636; and 8100 Old 13 Mile (e. of Van Dyke),
Warren, 574-9200. Carryout only: 4264 N. Wood-
ward (6 blks. n. of 13 Mile), Royal Oak, 549-8000;
and 14156 E. 12 Mile (bet. Schoenherr & Hayes),
Warren, 777-3400.   ☆ ☆ ☆

Buhl Cafe Bar
in Buhl Building, 2615 W. Congress (bet. Shelby &
Woodward), Detroit. 961-8911. L,D. $$
Known for Maurice salads and Buhl burgers, though
light menu stretches to broiled whitefish and fried
perch. Black banquettes and framed French prints
create French cafe scene.   ☆

Busia's
324 W. Main, Gaylord. (517) 732-2790. B,L,D. $
Friendly Polish cafe specializes in czarnina (duck's
blood soup), pierogi, potato pancakes, and kielbasa.
                                              ☆ ☆

Byblos
12967 Woodward (3 blks. s. of Davison), Highland
Park. 867-0923. L,D. $$
Intimate Lebanese eatery thrives despite a changing
neighborhood that's no longer Middle Eastern.
Good lamb chops, delicious shrimp with fresh cori-
ander, spicy falafel, and all the required parsley and
tahini appetizers.   ☆ ☆

Cadieux Cafe
4300 Cadieux (bet. Mack & E. Warren), Detroit.
882-8560. D. $$
Ex-Belgian nationals still flock here to swap bicy-
cling stories and do some feather bowling. Moun-
tains of mussels, homey mashed potatoes laced with
spinach, rabbit dinners, steamed jumbo shrimps,
and wonderful fried perch. Belgian beer, too.   ☆ ☆

Cafe Bon Homme

844 Penniman (1/2 blk. off Main), Plymouth.
453-6260. L,D. $$$$

A hidden little prize, accessible from gift and craft
shop. Intimate, nicely appointed tables await high-
styled American dishes: salmon poached in white
wine, smoked chicken pasta, and pheasant ravioli.
House-made desserts include chocolate pate with
Grand Marnier sauce, cheesecake, and a white chocolate cup filled with white chocolate mousse and
raspberry sauce.   ☆ ☆ ☆

Cafe Cortina

30715 W. 10 Mile (bet. Middlebelt & Orchard Lake),
Farmington Hills. 474-3033. L,D. $$$

Deluxe Italian dining. Amenities include comfy fire-
place setting, formal service, home-baked breads
and vegetables grown in adjacent garden. Specialties
are Vitello alla Cortina (veal layered with eggplant
and prosciutto), Vitello alla Capricciosa (veal sau-
teed with capers and olives), and Scampi alla Cor-
tina (prawns cooked in garlic and white wine).

☆ ☆ ☆

Cafe du Voyageur

205 W. Portage (at Ridge), Sault Ste. Marie.
(906) 632-0228. B,L,D. $$

Servers' outfits and setting recreate earlier days of
voyageurs on the St. Marys River. At dinner, whitefish, frog legs, scallops, steak, chicken cordon bleu.
Lunch recommendations are broccoli salad and
Finnish vegetable soup.

Cafe Jardin

in Somerset Mall, 2815 W. Big Beaver (at Coolidge),
Troy. 649-1348. L,D. $$

Where chic shoppers do lunch. Chicken pate with
basil and pecans, chicken quesadillas, fresh-baked
croissant sandwiches, and a terrific Caesar salad.
Interesting wines by the glass.   ☆ ☆

Sommelier is just a fancy name for wine steward. Three
of the most notable ones in Detroit are Madeline Triffon
of the London Chop House, Claudia Tyagi of The Whit-
ney, and Bob Campbell of the Westin Hotel.

The term "American bistro" has little to do with its
French counterpart, except the atmosphere is casual and
prices moderate.

Cafe Le Chat
17001 Kercheval (at Notre Dame), Grosse Pointe.
884-9077. L,D. $$$
Eastside gem in rear of Merry Mouse gourmet food
shop. French-country appointments are suited to an
always creative American menu which changes
monthly. Popular dishes include marinated Amish
chicken breast with tomato salsa on bed of black
beans; sauteed brook trout in black walnut crust;
sea scallops with avocado and roasted red pepper
butter. Precision desserts and Grosse Pointe wine
list. That means you'll find the Chardonnays and
Cabernets of Detroit's native son Fred Fisher (grand-
dad was one of the famous "Body by Fisher" brothers).
☆ ☆ ☆ ☆

Cafe Piccirilli
52830 Van Dyke (s. of 24 Mile), Utica. 731-0610.
L,D. $$$
Valet parking, stuffy waiters, starched linen and
strolling musicians (not to mention a dynamite
Saltimbocca alla Romano) add up to one of
Macomb Cty.'s fanciest eateries. Serious Italian fare:
sturdy homemade gnocchi, heaping portions of
basil-scented roasted peppers, Caesar salad at tableside and a lengthy list of veal dishes. Make your
house payment before you go. ☆ ☆

Cafe Rio
Westin Hotel, Renaissance Center, Detroit.
568-8201. B,L,D. $$
Casual Tex-Mex eatery on Promenade Level. Salad
bar and self-serve taco station streamline service.
Burritos, catfish with corn fritters, enchiladas, and
sizzling fajitas. ☆ ☆

Cajun Quarter, The
3236 Sandwich (at Mill), Windsor, Ontario.
(519) 258-8604. L,D. $$$
Cajun trend may be winding down elsewhere, but
it's going strong here. Smart, mostly pink dining
room with splashes of New Orleans posters. Shrimp
creole, blackened prime rib, seafood gumbo, jambalaya, and luscious sweet potato-pecan pie. Crawfish
tails are imported from Louisiana. ☆ ☆

Carl's Chop House
3020 Grand River (at Lodge Fwy.), Detroit.
833-0700. L,D. $$$
A Detroit institution: some of the biggest and best
steaks in town, the stoutest drinks for the dollar,
and no-nonsense service by waitresses with double-
digit seniority. Known for 30-ounce porterhouse.
Always open late; closed only on Christmas, which
also happens to be founder Carl Rosenfield's birthday.
☆ ☆ ☆

Carlucci
501 Pleasant (at Lake Blvd.), St. Joseph.
(616) 983-6535. L,D. Sun. Brunch. $$$
Under new owner, former Newberryport Cafe is
now totally redecorated to fit upscale southern Italian theme. Top seller is seafood fettucine. Manicotti,
veal, venison, and stone crab claws flown in from
Florida. New outdoor cafe with view of Lake
Michigan.

Caterings Cafe
102 Park W. (at Pellisier), Windsor, Ontario.
(519) 973-5577. B,L,D. $
Windsor's best coffee and muffin break. Favorites
are carrot-nut, peach, and mandarin. Neat little spot
is mainly carryout, but has plenty of tables. Turkey
waldorf salad, pasta primavera, Caesar salad, vegetables vinaigrette, plus daily hot dishes. (Closes at
7 p.m.) ☆ ☆

Caucus Club
150 W. Congress (bet. Woodward & Shelby),
Detroit. 965-4970. L,D. $$$
New York-style grill complete with live entertain-
ment nightly at the piano bar. Clubby, masculine
atmosphere is complemented by manly Texas chili,
marvelous baby back ribs, filet of Dover sole, and a
mountainous Caesar salad. ☆ ☆ ☆

Charley's Crab
at Crooks and I-75 (attached to Northfield Hilton),
Troy. 879-2060. L,D. $$$
Old Detroit elegance twinned with maritime memo-
rabilia. The result is a lovely setting for complex
seafood dishes. Norwegian salmon en papillote,
Florida grouper in lime-ginger beurre blanc, and red
snapper in gorgonzola cream. Key lime pie is the
real thing. ☆ ☆ ☆

Charley's Seafood Taverns
L,D. $$

Chain of locally owned casual family restaurants, specializing in seafood and pasta. Bloomfield Charley's, 5656 W. Maple (at Orchard Lake), West Bloomfield, 855-2244; Northville Charley's, 41122 W. 7 Mile (w. of Haggerty), Northville, 349-9220; Eastside Charley's, 19265 Vernier (across from Eastland Center), Harper Woods, 884-2811; Southfield Charley's, 19701 W. 12 Mile (e. of Evergreen), Southfield, 559-4400; Fairlane Charley's, 700 Town Center (at Fairlane Town Center), Dearborn, 336-8550; Livonia Charley's, 31501 Schoolcraft (at Merriman), Livonia, 422-4550.   ☆ ☆

Charly's Tavern
4715 Tecumseh E. (at Pillette), Windsor, Ontario. (519) 945-5512. L,D. $

First brew-pub in Windsor. Homemade beer is called Timeout. There are two styles: a German-style lager or "dry." No food, but a window connects bar to a next-door pizzeria.

Chesaning Heritage House
605 W. Broad (M-57), Chesaning. (517) 845-7700. L,D. $$$

Turn-of-the-century Southern-style mansion converted to Americana restaurant. House specialty is stuffed pork tenderloin. Prime rib, seafood, ice cream sundae pie. Meals begin with homemade cheese spread, garlic toast, and soup.

Chez Raphael
2700 Sheraton Dr. (at I-96 and Novi Rd.), Novi. 348-5555. D. $$$$

Dining doesn't get much better: elegant chateau setting, impeccable service, elevated Continental American cooking. Chef Ed Janos sees to the detailed dishes; Achille Bianchi to the dining room and mile-long wine list. Menu changes daily, but expect entrees like a split whole baby pheasant, boned, served over a warm beet vinaigrette with morel mushroom sauce, or tournedos of beef with leek flan and sauce of asparagus tips, roasted shallots, red pepper, and thyme.   ☆ ☆ ☆ ☆ ☆

Chez Vins Bistro Bistro

26 Chatham St. E., (bet. Goyeau & Ouellette),
Windsor, Ontario. (519) 252-2801. L,D. $$
Quiet, hip spot to take a date. (Or to spy on traffic
at classy strip joint across the street.) Stark decor is
accented with ultra-contemporary paintings. Black
bean cassoulet, grilled chicken with raspberry-Grand
Marnier sauce, lamb chops with mustard and rose-
mary. Marvelous broccoli soup capped with Cana-
dian cheddar. Best wine list in Windsor. Try the
Pelee Island whites.   ☆ ☆ ☆

Chicago Road House

21400 Michigan Ave. (w. of Southfield), Dearborn.
565-5710. L,D. $$$
Formal Loop Room and casual Windows on the
Rouge offer similar menus of steaks and seafood.
Coat, tie, and Gold Card recommended for the
Loop. Prime rib, filet mignon, New York strip,
Dover sole.   ☆ ☆

Clamdigger's

30555 Grand River (bet. Orchard Lake & Middle-
belt), Farmington Hills. 478-3800. L,D. $$$
Upscale seafood specialties, including new gimmick:
"hot rock" cooking. Guest cooks his own filet, lob-
ster, shrimp, or fish at the table on preheated pol-
ished granite rock. Dipping sauces and side vegeta-
bles included.

Clarkston Cafe

18 S. Main (bet. Depot & Washington), Clarkston.
625-5660. L,D. $$$
Rustic country setting with American regional cook-
ing. Two-tiered menu offers wonderful soups, onion
rings, and sandwiches for casual eating, or a selec-
tion of entrees for the serious diner. Tournedos
Grand Duke, rack of lamb, and Veal Madagascar.
Dessert specialty is Half White Half Dark Chocolate
Pie.   ☆ ☆ ☆ ☆

Clementine's

418 Phoenix (bet. Kalamazoo St. & Center St.),
South Haven. (616) 637-4755. L,D. $
Families queue for tables at 1890s tavern. Beer-
steamed shrimp, onion rings "on a stick," burgers,
and a broiled crab and shrimp open-face sandwich
called (wouldn't you know?) "Oh my darling."

Clementine's Too

*1235 Broad St. (across from Pier 33 Marina), St.
Joseph. (616) 983–0990. L,D. $$*

Huge, open warehouse-type building looks nothing
like the Clementine's in South Haven. Weighty spe-
cialties are 16-ounce Kansas City strip steak and a
64-ounce salad.

Cloverleaf Bar & Restaurant

*24443 Gratiot (s. of 10 Mile), East Detroit.
777–5391. L,D. Sun. Brunch. $$*

Site of pizza history: Late owner Gus Guerra originated the recipe for square, deep-dish pizza when he
owned Buddy's Rendezvous back in the 1940s. Cloverleaf's sprawling family tavern populated by
couples, kids, and baseball teams—all with pepper-
oni on their chins.   ☆ ☆

Confetti's

*6480 Orchard Lake (at Maple), West Bloomfield.
626–3341. L,D. $$$*

Smart cafe and bar with emphasis on light Italian-
inspired cooking: Caesar salad, a dozen pasta
dishes, broiled seafood, a little chicken. Ice creams
are homemade. Hip wine list.   ☆ ☆ ☆

Cook's Shop/Pasta Shop

*683 Ouellette (bet. Wyandotte & Elliott), Windsor,
Ontario. (519) 254–3377. D. $$*

Both are Italian, but downstairs Cook's Shop is the
preferred room. Pastas and salads assembled at
tableside, aged steaks, excellent wine (owner usually
has special bottles that may or may not be on the
menu). Only problem is, it's so dark you can't find
your table. Hallmark dish is Spaghetti alla Chitarra
Carbonara flavored with lightly sauteed bacon and
wine. Upstairs Pasta Shop is more casual. Reservations mandatory.   ☆ ☆ ☆

Cooper's Arms

*306 Main (at Third St.), Rochester. 651–2266. L,D.
$$$*

A mainstay of downtown Rochester with light menu
in the lounge, full array of seafood and steaks in the
dining room. Known for whitefish a la Oscar and
frog legs. A special heart-healthy menu was devel-
oped with the help of Oakland University.   ☆

Country Epicure
42050 Grand River (bet. Meadowbrook & Novi Rd.), Novi. 349-7770. L,D. $$
More contemporary than country. Totally remodeled eatery now has solarium, outdoor seating and new trimmed-down menu. Lots of grilled and broiled fish, heavenly corn bread sticks glazed with sugar and nuts, plus a wondrous dessert tray. Surpasses expectations.   ☆ ☆ ☆

Country Jim's
4743 Dixie Hwy., (at Williams Lake Rd.), Drayton Plains. 674-4815. B,L,D. $
Knotty-pine decor feels Michigan, but menu is strictly Southern: fried catfish, chicken and dumplings, pinto beans, corn bread, and barbecued pork. At breakfast, hot biscuits and gravy, Kentucky-cured ham, American fries, and old-fashioned buckwheat pancakes.   ☆ ☆

Cousin Jenny's Cornish Pasties
111 W. Front and 510 W. 14th, Traverse City. (616) 941-7821, (616) 946-3085. L,D. $
Famous meat pies of Upper Peninsula are available hot or partially baked. The "original" contains steak, rutabaga, onions, and potatoes; six other varieties are available. Also offered: 24 "outrageous" flavors of cheesecake. Limited seating; mostly carryouts.
☆ ☆ ☆

Cousins Heritage Inn
7954 Ann Arbor St., Dexter (Exit 167 off I-94). 426-3020. L,D. $$$
Serious cooking steams up 19th century house. Owner Paul Cousins sees to desserts such as flourless chocolate tortes, iced souffles and fresh raspberry tarts, while chef Greg Upschur provides weekly changing entrees like wild game, poached salmon in lobster sauce, or veal roulade stuffed with pork and veal mousses. Upschur welcomes vegetarians, especially if they call ahead. Pat Cousins is hostess.   ☆ ☆ ☆ ☆

Crispigna's
1213 Ludington (bet. 12th & 13th), Escanaba. (906) 786-8660. D. $$
Some consider this the best Italian food in the U.P. Homemade pasta, lasagna, steak.

Cucina Di Pasta
in The Boardwalk, 6887 Orchard Lake (at Maple),
West Bloomfield. 626–9210. L,D. $$
Trendy Italian carryout with handful of tables and
tempting showcase of prepared salads, sauces, and
homemade pastas. Some are cholesterol-free.
Espresso and cappucino. ☆ ☆

Cuisine de Pays
at Van Dyke Place, 649 Van Dyke (off E. Jeffer-
son), Detroit. 821–2620. D. $$
Elegant Van Dyke Place's casual country-French
eatery in the lower-level billiards room. Dishes available in appetizer or entree sizes. Beet and watercress
salad, bouillabaisse, chilled marinated halibut filet
with couscous, venison bourguignonne in gougere,
goujonettes of chicken with fresh figs and orzo.

☆ ☆ ☆ ☆

Cygnus
Amway Grand Plaza Hotel, 187 Pearl (at Monroe),
Grand Rapids. (616) 776-6425. D. $$$
All-glass restaurant on the 28th floor showcases
some of the most elaborate cooking in Southwest
Michigan. Thick venison medallions topped with
foie gras, tender scaloppini of duckling in cider
sauce, and signature gin tomato soup cooked table-
side. Artificial white palm trees surround the band
and dance floor. Very dark, very intimate, very
wicked. ☆ ☆ ☆ ☆

D. Dennison's Seafood Tavern
27909 Orchard Lake (at 12 Mile), Farmington Hills.
553-7000. L,D. $$
Casual, family eatery provides full array of shellfish
and seafood supplemented with chicken, pastas,
sandwiches, and salads. Raw bar; changing daily
seafood specials. Deliciously thick New England
seafood chowder. ☆ ☆

D.J. Kelly's
120 Park (bet. State & Front St.), Traverse City.
(616) 941-4550. L,D. $$
Casual, contemporary eatery bills its food as "nou-
veau" Midwestern cuisine, which means smoked
salmon croissants, "boboli" pizza topped with sau-
teed duck and havarti cheese, and grilled dark meat
of chicken with tomato and purple onion relish.
Michigan wines by the glass. ☆ ☆

Da Edoardo

19767 Mack (at Cook Rd.), Grosse Pointe Woods.
881–8540. D. $$$
Fine Northern Italian-style cooking in keeping with
the conservative but sterling values of Grosse Pointe.
Quiet, intimate atmosphere. Pasta, seafood, and
veal. Delicious Bolognese sauce, minestrone, and
main course called Veal Alicia. Adjacent trattoria
offers more moderately priced pizza, pasta, and
simple main courses. Serious Italian wine list in
both.   ☆ ☆ ☆ ☆

Da Luciano

1317 Hall Rd. (at Ottawa), Windsor, Ontario.
(519) 977–5677. L,D. $$
Yet another Windsor hideaway for chianti and can-
neloni. Chef-operated eatery means Luciano Verardi
keeps a watchful eye on not just the kitchen, but
also the dining room. He's often seen at tables
checking on guests' enjoyment of the fettucine
Alfredo, stracciatella soup, or Scaloppine alla
Luciano (veal in cream sauce with mushrooms). ☆ ☆

Dakota Inn Rathskeller

17324 John R (2 blks. n. of 6 Mile), Detroit.
867–9722. L,D. $$
Beer hall setting and sing-alongs make up for the
limited menu. Food is mostly German — knackwurst,
smoked pork chops, red cabbage, and potato salad.
Perfect meeting place for large groups.   ☆

Dam Site Inn

U.S. 31 (1 1/2 mi. s. of Pellston), Pellston.
(616) 539–8851. D. $$$
All-you-can-eat family-style chicken dinners, includ-
ing homemade noodles, mashed potatoes, gravy,
vegetables, relish, and biscuits and honey. A la carte
menu offers steak and seafood. Kitchen is so clean
that tours are welcomed. Noted for hospitality.
Open from late April to late October.   ☆ ☆

Most entrees:	No stars	Not Rated
$ = less than $7	☆	Good
$$ = $7 to $13	☆ ☆	Very Good
$$$ = $13 to $19	☆ ☆ ☆	Excellent
$$$$ = $19 or more	☆ ☆ ☆ ☆	Outstanding
	☆ ☆ ☆ ☆ ☆	Superb
See p. xi for explanations.		

Danny's Bar & Grill

225 Jos. Campau (at Jefferson), Detroit. 259-3675.
L,D. $

A swinging spot in Rivertown, especially on hot
summer nights when the outdoor deck is open.
Inside, a marvelous '50s-style bar and tables covered
with white linen. Trendy burgers, creative salads,
and daily specials such as lake trout with red pepper
sauce and boneless almond chicken. Assorted bottled beers.   ☆ ☆

Dearborn Inn

20301 Oakwood (bet. Michigan & Rotunda), Dear-
born. 271-2700. B,L,D. Sun. Brunch. $$$

Marriott's $25-million restoration of Henry Ford's
original airport hotel preserves Georgian elegance of
Early American Room while updating menu to cur-
rent American cooking. Smoked seafood sampler,
grilled chicken in champagne sauce, prime rib, fresh
lake perch. Remodeled Ten Eyck Tavern offers
casual salads, pastas, and sandwiches. Great break-
fast of Belgian waffles and bracing coffee.   ☆ ☆ ☆

Dearborn Tavern

22145 W. Outer Drive (at Pelham), Dearborn.
563-5211. L,D. $$

Surprisingly fancy menu for a neighborhood bar &
grill. Shrimp Alfredo, swordfish steak, and grilled
pickerel, besides burgers and the usual bar grub.
All-you-can-eat crab legs on Tuesdays, and steaks
priced at $8.95 on Thursdays. Even a respectable
wine list.   ☆ ☆

Del Rio

122 W. Washington (at S. Ashley), Ann Arbor.
761-2530. L,D. $

More popular with nostalgic baby boomers and
leftover hippies than college kids. Known for Del
Rio "Det" burger that's smothered with mushrooms,
black olives, green pepper, and onions steamed in
beer. Soups are vegetarian; so are the Mexican
dishes.

Reservations, especially at the finer restaurants, are mandatory on weekends. In booking a table in advance, ask
the name of the reservation taker. Just in case.

Best wine buys on local restaurant lists are usually from
Argentina, Chile, Spain, or Michigan.

Deli Unique
in West Bloomfield Plaza, 6724 Orchard Lake Rd.
(at Maple), West Bloomfield. 737-3890. L,D. Sun.
Brunch. $
Unique because a bona fide chef in white coat and
checked pants runs the kitchen. (Usually, delis don't
get that fancy.) Who would expect Caesar salad,
grilled chicken with basil-red pepper butter, and
ground turkey burgers? Known for cheese blintzes;
famous for sour cream coffeecake. Also at 25290
Greenfield, n. of 10 Mile, Oak Park, 967-3999. ☆ ☆

DePalma's Restaurant
31735 Plymouth (w. of Merriman), Livonia.
261-2430. L,D. $$
A cut above the typical Italian family restaurant.
Homemade soups, breads and pastas. Provimi veal
and shrimp are on the high end; gnocchi and meat-
balls on the low. Fluffy cheesecake with ladyfinger
crust is specialty. Vito DePalma built his reputation
at Clairpointe in Grosse Pointe.   ☆ ☆

Desmond's
in The Drawbridge Inn, 283 N. Christina St. (at
George), Sarnia, Ontario. (519) 337-7571. B,L,D.
Sun. Brunch. $$$
French-Italian cooking convenient to the harbor.
Chicken Piccata, scallops Florentine, prime rib.
Weekend Italian buffet.

Diana's Delight
143 W. Main (e. of Otsego St.), Gaylord.
(517) 732-6564. B,L. $
New jolt of creativity is welcomed by townspeople.
Contemporary, light American cooking with "skillet
breakfasts" (sauteed crumbled sausage, green pepper,
and onion with two eggs any style), eggs benedict on
grilled croissant with herbed hollandaise, deli sandwiches, and homemade soups. Fresh-baked cinnamon rolls and jumbo muffins. (Open 7 a.m. to 4
p.m.)

Dill's Olde Town
423 S. Union, Traverse City. (616) 947-7534. L,D.
$$
Traverse City's oldest restaurant and meeting place.
Light lunches of salads and deli sandwiches; more
serious dinner menu of perch, whitefish, spareribs,
and prime rib.   ☆ ☆

Dogpatch, The

25 E. Superior (off M-28), Munising.
(906) 387-9948. B,L,D. Sun. Brunch. $$
Restaurant, lounge, and gift shop cater mainly to
snowmobilers. Decor is L'il Abner theme. Big coun-
try breakfast; the rest of the day, there's a salad bar
and seafood buffet, plus a la carte menu. "You'll
never leave here hungry," boasts owner Bill Ramsey,
who also operates nearby snowmobile dealership.

Don Carlos Mexican Restaurante

13701 W. Warren (at Schaefer), Dearborn.
582-2024. L,D. $$
Every time you look, a new one is opening up. But
no wonder: menus are more adventuresome than
most family Mexican eateries. Mussels, fajitas, pan-
fried red snapper, plus all the regular eats. Other
locations: 7034 Middlebelt (s. of Warren), Garden
City, 458-2900; 33025 Gratiot (at 14 Mile), Mt.
Clemens, 791-9120; 2542 Oakwood (2 blks. e. of
Dix), Melvindale, 388-8451; 415 E. Congress (e. of
Woodward), Detroit, 961-5005; 9565 Telegraph (at
W. Chicago), Redford Twp., 533-8000.   ☆ ☆

Double Eagle

5725 Rochester Rd. (at Square Lake Rd.), Troy.
879-1555. L,D. Sun. Brunch. $$$
Comfortable, glassed dining room overlooks rolling,
wooded fairways of Sylvan Glen Golf Course.
Trendy American regional dishes: loin of Michigan
pork with morel mushrooms, Indiana free-range
chicken with pancetta and garlic, grilled Florida
swordfish with plum tomatoes and olives.   ☆ ☆ ☆

Ducks on the Roof

Hwy. 18, (2 mi. w. of Amhurstburg, 35 min. drive
from the border), Ontario. (519) 736-6555 or
(Detroit number) 961-3228. D. $$$
Pine tables, a cozy fireplace and too many duck
decoys to count create warm setting in rural
Ontario. New owners have upgraded eatery's traditional Continental-style cooking. Boneless breast of
free-range pheasant with wild mushrooms, coho
salmon in champagne-raspberry sauce, rack of lamb,
and roast rabbit brushed with Dijon mustard. Entree
price includes soup, steamed vegetable, bread, and
potato.

Dunleavy'z River Place

267 Jos Campau (bet. Jefferson & Franklin),
Detroit. 259-0909. L,D. $$
If bars are an art form, this is the Mona Lisa.
Lively city saloon that's found a home with nearby
Stroh folk as well as GP'ers and downtown office
workers. Hard to imagine a meatier hamburger or
tastier homemade onion rings. Known for ribs. Also
at 34505 Grand River, Farmington, 478-8866. ☆ ☆ ☆

Dusty's Wine Bar & Pub

in Galleria shopping plaza, 1839 Grand River (just
e. of Marsh Rd.), Okemos. (517) 349-5150. L,D.
Sun. Brunch. $$
Creative bistro dishes with more serious implications
than their tame names imply, i.e. the Bolivian Macaroni and Torta Rustica. Eclectic menu offers grilled
marlin with avocado-corn relish, roast Michigan
pheasant with dried cherry butter, plus sandwiches
on sourdough. Breads, mayonnaise, and catsup are
homemade. More than a dozen wines by the glass,
200 by the bottle, plus 80 beers. ☆ ☆ ☆

E.G. Nick's

6066 W. Maple (e. of Farmington Rd.), West
Bloomfield. 851-0805. L,D. $$
Bustling family tavern with top-notch ribs, roast
chicken, pasta, fresh fish, hearth-baked pizza, and a
dynamite Greek salad. ☆ ☆

Earle, The

121 W. Washington (at Ashley), Ann Arbor.
994-0211. D. $$$
Large cellar eatery focuses on country French and
country Italian dishes: medallions of lamb with
garlic, tomato and olives; sauteed salmon with fresh
sorrel; duck pate, and shrimp baked in parchment.
Famous for wine list, some 800 labels strong. ☆ ☆ ☆

Eddie's Drive-In

36111 Jefferson (at Ballard), Mt. Clemens.
469-2345. L,D. $
What a hoot. Food hardly matters, though it's not
bad. (In case you're wondering, it's a hot dog joint.)
What does matter are your wheels — your car, man!
On summer weekends, vintage auto clubs slate meet-
ings in the parking lot. Keep eyes peeled for roller-
skating waitresses. ☆

El Gaucho
9411 Telegraph (s. of Wick), Taylor. 291-0555. L,D. $$
It's amazing how pleasant an old Clock restaurant can look when you dress it in a south-of-the-border theme. Menu is partly Argentinian: empanadas (meat pies), Milanesa de Pollo (breaded breast of chicken); Costeleta a Caballo (grilled steak topped with fried eggs); Asado (barbecued short ribs or chicken). The rest is Mexican: tacos, enchiladas, tostadas, burritos. ☆

El Zocalo Mexican Restaurant
3400 Bagley (at 23rd St.), Detroit. 841-3700. L,D. $
Owners Victor and Yvonne Cordoba offer more upscale Mexican decor than neighboring spots, but the menu is still basically everything you'd hope to find in Mexican Town. ☆ ☆

Elaine's
in Hotel Pontchartrain, 2 Washington Blvd. (at Jefferson), Detroit. 965-0200. B,L,D. Sun. Brunch. $$$
Upscale dining room is still searching for identity. Predictable perch, pasta, and veal at dinner; specials are more in the contemporary American/French vein. ☆ ☆

Elizabeth Street Cafe
2100 John R (at Elizabeth), Detroit. 964-0461. B,L. $
A boon for nearby Detroit College of Law students. Attractions are breakfasts of homemade apple-cinnamon rolls, homey omelets, and hearty coffee, followed by lunches of spicy black bean soup and curried chicken salad. Specialty sandwiches and four soups every day. ☆ ☆

Elizabeth's by the Lake
23722 Jefferson (at 9 Mile), St. Clair Shores. 775-3700. L,D. Sun. Brunch. $$
Where ladies do lunch, gents retire to the bar. Miles of mauve, sky lights, and white tablecloths are stage for everything from veal Oscar and prime rib to wing dings and potato skins. A bit unfocused, but at least there's variety. ☆

Elwood Bar and Grill
2100 Woodward (at Elizabeth), Detroit. 961-7485.
L,D. $$
Totally restored art deco bar & grill across from Fox
Theatre gives new meaning to American diner food:
flavored fresh whipped potatoes, green beans with
the tips intact, and veal meatloaf heaped with wild
mushroom gravy. Even a wonderful homemade
tomato soup. Nerves of steel are required to endure
thumping '50s jukebox, but that's just part of the
fun.   ☆ ☆ ☆

Embers, The
1217 S. Mission (at Preston), Mt. Pleasant.
(517) 773-5007. L,D. Sun. Brunch. $$$
Thirty-year-old institution known for 1-pound pork
chop, prime rib, and the house pea & peanut salad.
Dinners include relish tray, salad, potato, and homemade rolls. Famous Sunday brunch.

Epicurean Cafe
645 Griswold, lower level of Penobscot Building,
Detroit. 965-4998. B,L. $
Especially handy if you're downtown on jury duty
or work in the vicinity. Cafeteria with variety of
home-cooked hot entrees, interesting salads and deli
sandwiches. Also located on lower level of First
Federal Building, at Michigan and Woodward, in
downtown Detroit, 964-2230.   ☆ ☆

Escoffier
in the Bell Tower Hotel, 300 S. Thayer (at Washing-
ton), Ann Arbor. 995-3800. L,D. $$$
European-flavored dining room with classic French
cooking and nationally recognized wine list. Owner-
chef Tony Perault keeps menu brief but focused:
excellent soups (mushroom is a specialty) and excep-
tional salads complementing a half-dozen main
courses. Wife Maureen sees to the wine list, strong
in older vintages of California Chardonnay. ☆ ☆ ☆ ☆

Q—What restaurant in Detroit also is a licensed dairy? (It
makes its own cheese and ice cream). A—Traffic Jam &
Snug.

If you're a vegetarian and dining at an upscale restaurant,
it is sometimes best to call ahead and alert the chef. That
way you might get something special.

Evergreen Grill, The

327 Abbott Rd. (off Grand River), E. Lansing.
(517) 337–1200. B,L,D. Sun. Brunch. $$

Original E. Lansing post office converted to contemporary restaurant. Health-conscious kitchen produces a mix of traditional American dishes — chicken pot pie and planked whitefish — plus more trendy black bean salsa with blue corn tortilla chips. Sunday brunch menu shows the breadth: egg tacos; cornmeal pancakes with apple compote; smoked turkey, spinach and a poached egg in Mornay sauce stacked on an English muffin.   ☆ ☆ ☆

Excalibur

28875 Franklin Rd. (at Northwestern Hwy.),
Southfield. 358–3355. L,D. $$$

Las Vegas supperclub atmosphere lures affluent martini toters who demand raw-in-the-center steaks and broiled fish with the sauce on the side. Sinatra, a customer when he's in town, says the baby back ribs are done "my way."   ☆ ☆ ☆

Fairfield's

in the Sterling Inn, 34911 Van Dyke (at 15 Mile
Rd.), Sterling Heights. 979–1420. B,L,D. Sun.
Brunch. $$$

Some of the best food in Macomb Cty., and all the Van Dyke auto execs know it. Atmosphere may not exactly bowl you over, but check that food: marvelous homemade dill rolls, rich crabcakes garnished with caviar-dotted lemons, fabulous chicken Forestier in a white wine-Dijon sauce. Homemade desserts, premium wine. Quality and value are the bottom line.   ☆ ☆ ☆

Farm House, The

1128 E. 9 Mile (bet. John R & Dequindre), Hazel
Park. 541–2132. L,D. $$$

Old-fashioned hospitality begins with relishes and ends with French silk chocolate pie. Fran and Mary Trambush carry on their late mom's traditions, which date from 1934. Lamb shanks, short ribs, roast pork, roast veal, and baked breast of chicken. Known for pies: raspberry, sour cream apple, cherry-berry.   ☆ ☆

Finney's Pub
3965 Woodward (at Alexandrine), Detroit.
831-8070. L,D. $
Respectable saloon in the shadow of the Medical
Center. Meshes menu of Mexican nibbles with typical bar eats. ☆

Fischer's Happy Hour Tavern
M-22 (midway bet. Leland & Northport),
Northport. (616) 386-9923. L,D. $
A gem of a hamburger joint that only local residents
seem to know about. Old summer home converted
to a family tavern is where everybody meets for a
burger, fries, and bowl of homemade soup. Old oak
tables, Bentwood chairs, and checkered place mats
testify to many years of family ownership. ☆ ☆

Fox & Hounds
1560 N. Woodward (at Long Lake), Bloomfield
Hills. 644-4800. L,D. $$$
More traditional than trendy, though chef Terry
Schuster tries to broaden the experience. Specialties
are porterhouse steaks, barbecued salmon with Gulf
shrimp, and sauteed perch in Parmesan-breadcrumb
coating with tomatoes, artichokes, and capers.
Extensive wine list. Bar scene is middle-age
crazy. ☆ ☆ ☆

Franconian Restaurant, The
in Bavarian Inn Motor Lodge, 1 Covered Bridge
Lane, Frankenmuth. (517) 652-2651, ext. 509.
B,L,D. Sun. Brunch. $$
German-American specialties, but best known for
Sunday brunch buffet with six major food stations.
Hot entrees include carved roast beef, smoked ham,
fried chicken, and baked fish. Brunch hours are 11
a.m. to 2 p.m.

Frankenmuth Corner Tavern and Restaurant
100 S. Main (at Junction Rd.), Frankenmuth.
(517) 652-8171. B,L,D. $
Where the local people eat. Famous for breakfast
(omelets, waffles, pancakes) and perch dinners.
Seven homemade soups, plus Frankenmuth beer. A
real find if you're tired of chicken dinners. ☆ ☆

French Market Cafe

216 S. Fourth (bet. Liberty & Washington), Ann Arbor. 761–6200. B,L,D. Sun. Brunch. $

Earnest attempt at New Orleans cooking, including beignets, cafe au lait, red beans and rice with ham, jambalaya, a hearty gumbo, and sweet potato pie. At breakfast, a muffuletta sandwich, eggs Florentine and Benedict, fresh strawberry crepes, and po' boy sandwiches (oyster and turkey). There's more to this little white storefront than meets the eye.   ☆ ☆

Galley, The

241 N. State (off I-75), St. Ignace. (906) 643–7960. B,L,D. $$

Overlooks Lake Huron with view of Mackinac Island. Famous for broiled whitefish and sauteed whitefish livers. Lake trout, deep-fried lake perch, steak, prime rib. Children's and seniors' menus available. Open mid-May to mid-October.

Galligan's

519 E. Jefferson (at Beaubien), Detroit. 963–2098. L,D. $$

Popular lunch and after-work spot, especially on the upper-floor deck. Trendy eats such as black bean soup, specialty sandwiches (the "Alpha" and "Jazzwich"), chicken and shrimp specials daily, and fresh fish. Assorted bottled beers.   ☆ ☆

Gandy Dancer

401 Depot (bet. State & Main), Ann Arbor. 769–0592. L,D. Sun. Brunch. $$$

Seafood of every shape and shell, but real attraction is the setting in an old, historic train station. Mussels a la Muer, Charley's Chowder, and great home-made garlic rolls are clues: this happens to be a Chuck Muer restaurant.   ☆ ☆ ☆

Genitti's Hole in the Wall

104 E. Main (bet. Center & Hutton), Northville. 349–0522. L,D. $ (Lunch); $$$$ (Dinner)

Light-hearted Italian spot that really does amount to a hole in the wall if you check the square feet. Fans, though, take the food seriously. A popular half sandwich and soup (with cheesecake dessert) for $5.29 at lunch and family-style Italian dinner ($19.39 all-inclusive) at night.

Ginopolis' on the Grill

27815 Middlebelt (at 12 Mile), Farmington Hills.
851–8222. L,D. $$
Previous singles spot may have switched to casual
dinner house theme geared to families, but sports
stars still hang out here. Display kitchen with char-
grill. Large variety of fresh fish plus pasta, barbe-
cued ribs, chicken. Also at 2273 Crooks Rd., Roch-
ester, 853–7333.   ☆ ☆ ☆

Giovanni's

330 S. Oakwood (w. of Fort), Detroit. 841–0122.
L,D. $$$
What started out as a place for simple, home-style
Italian cooking (manicotti, canneloni, delicious
pizza) grew sophisticated fast. All the expected
veals—piccante and Marsala—but also Cappelletti
Verde (small spinach raviolis filled with veal, cream
cheese and ricotta); Angel Hair Pomodore (thin
pasta in fresh tomato sauce); Lasagna Primavera
(layered with vegetables). Warm Italian hospitality,
serious Italian wine list.   ☆ ☆ ☆

Giulio & Sons

in Dearborn Hyatt Regency, Fairlane Town Center,
Dearborn. 593–1234. L,D. Sun. Brunch. $$$
Lavish Sunday brunch and daily "market stand"
buffet of antipasto salads, meats, pastas, soups, and
garlic breads have been trademarks since Day One.
Rest of the menu follows Italian theme: crabmeat
fettucine, chicken carbonara, and shrimp oreganata.
For real meat-eaters, there's a 22-ounce porterhouse
with sauteed mushrooms.   ☆ ☆

Glen Lake Inn

4566 Cty. Rd. 616, Maple City. (616) 334–3587.
L,D. $$$
Maybe off the beaten track, but people have known
about Hochstein's wiener schnitzel and sauerbraten
for years. The chocolate-brown frame house with
bright-red tablecloths, black banquettes, and dim
lighting specializes in German cooking but also
offers updated American dishes: seared turkey
breast tenderloin in mushroom-leek cream, roast
pheasant with apples, and salmon in champagne-dill
sauce. (Seasonal hours.)   ☆

Gnome, The
4120 Woodward (bet. Alexandrine & Willis),
Detroit. 833-0120. L,D. Sun. Brunch. $$
Artsy crowd streams in for full menu of Middle
Eastern specialties mixed with a pinch of American.
Popular before and after-theatre spot. Entertainment.

☆ ☆

Golden Galleon
624 Third (s. of Fort), Detroit. 961-2060. L,D. $
Media hangout, but proximity to Joe Louis Arena
makes it a perfect grub stop for Wings fans, too.
Hamburgers, sandwiches, salads, pan-fried pickerel,
New York strip.

☆

Golden Grill, The
M-28, Seney. (906) 499-3323. B,L,D. $
Mennonite-owned family restaurant noted for home-
made pasties, salad bar at noon (includes meat and
potatoes), and smorgasbord at dinner. Homemade
cinnamon rolls and pies. Traveling east across the
U.P., this is the last major eating spot before the
"Seney stretch."

Golden Mushroom
18100 W. 10 Mile (at Southfield), Southfield.
559-4230. L,D. $$$$
Upstairs: The ultimate in dining. Certified master
chef Milos Cihelka offers impeccable Continental
cuisine with service, wine, and fine table appoint-
ments to match. Imported caviar, sauteed foie gras,
wild mushrooms in puff pastry, and game dishes
have no match. Wine list with depth and breadth. A
"health special" at lunch and dinner. This room is
for the connoisseur. Downstairs: $$ More casual
Mushroom Cellar offers extensive lunch menu
including "upstairs" specials at slightly reduced prices
plus Maurice salad, soups, burgers, beef tips, and
tuna croissant. At dinner, fresh pizzas, lamb kebabs,
baked crabmeat toast.

☆ ☆ ☆ ☆ ☆

In descending order, the top Russian caviars are beluga,
osetra, and sevruga. As wine and caviar merchant Ed
Jonna says, just remember the acronym BOS.

When figuring the gratuity, some people base the amount
on food costs only. It is more customary, however, to tip
on the bottom line.

Govinda's
at the Fisher Mansion, Bhaktivedanta Cultural Center, 383 Lenox (off Jefferson), Detroit. 331–6740. L,D. $$
Opulent marble and onyx setting in former Lawrence Fisher estate. New owners, the Krishnas, have preserved and enhanced the early 20th century grandeur. Second floor dining room specializes in Indian, vegetarian, and international cuisines. Beautiful grounds. Reservations recommended. ☆ ☆

Grain Train
421 Howard (1 blk. s. of Mitchell), Petoskey. (616) 347–2381. $
Dairy-free vegetarian co-op has self-serve deli. Seating is limited; mostly carryouts. Tofu salad, tempeh burgers, soy tapioca, and Mexican munchies such as burritos and nachos. Complete bakery with whole-grain breads, cookies, and muffins, including oat bran. ☆ ☆

Grand Hotel
Mackinac Island. (906) 847–3331. B,L,D. $$$$
Formal, buttercup-yellow dining room with white trim, blue ceiling and hardwood floors is nearly three-quarters the size of a football field (seats 600) and requires proper attire after 6 p.m. A sometimes-inspired menu of whitefish, prime rib, chicken, and veal. Signature dessert is the Grand pecan ball. Outsiders pay $40 for the five-course meal; if you are a guest in the hotel, meals are included in the price of the room. ☆ ☆

Grande Mere Inn
5800 Red Arrow Hwy., (Exit 22 off I-94), Stevensville. (616) 429–3591. L,D. $$
Great sunsets visible from west-facing windows on ridge above Lake Michigan. Owners Pete and Nancy Racine emphasize seafood (perch, scallops), with dash of lamb, ribs, steak. Homemade desserts include praline cheesecake.

Got a real complaint about dinner? See the owner or write him a letter. The best spots will always try to make things right. If all else fails, contact the local restaurant critic.

Don't for one second think the nightly special will be the least expensive item on the menu. Often, it's just the opposite. Ask the price.

Gratzi

326 S. Main (bet. E. Liberty & E. William), Ann Arbor. 663-5555. L,D. $$

Trendy food and sizzling atmosphere. Cuisine is Northern Italian: crusty bread, thin pizzas, grilled chicken, salads with an arsenal of radicchio, and steak smeared with gorgonzola. Parting glass of Sambuca or Frangelico is on the house. No reservations. ☆ ☆ ☆

Great Lakes Inn, The

9334 N. River Rd. (bet. Roberts Rd. & Sherwood Ln.), Algonac. 774-0900. L,D. $$$

White Georgian-style inn with new dining room overlooking swimming pool and tennis courts. White tablecloths and candles share table space with fork-tender filet mignon, charbroiled whitefish, lime-broiled chicken with mushrooms. Children's portions available.

Great Lakes Whitefish & Chips

411 Bridge, Charlevoix. (616) 547-4374. L,D. $

The name says it all: an unpretentious cafe/carryout where owner Terry Left can look out his window and see the fishing boats bringing in his No. 1 seller—whitefish. ☆ ☆

Grecian Gardens

562 Monroe (bet. St. Antoine & Beaubien), Detroit. 961-3044. L,D. $$

All the required Greek specialties, but owner Phillip Menas still has the corner on lamb chops. Large platter has six meaty ribs, plus salad and vegetable. Shish kebab is outstanding. ☆ ☆

Gyliane

1880 Wyandotte E. (at Kildare), Windsor, Ontario. (519) 256-8381. L,D. $$

So French-Canadian that waiters often inquire which language they should use. At lunch, traditional Canadian meat pies called tourtieres, puff pastry shells with savory fillings, pates, and quiche. At night, a more elaborate menu that includes rabbit.

☆ ☆

Haab's

18 W. Michigan (at Huron), Ypsilanti. 483–8200.
L,D. $$
Famous for prime rib, but today the 15 daily sea-
food items usually outsell it. This is an old-
fashioned restaurant, in business more than 50
years, that still peels potatoes for french fries, cracks
eggs to make mayonnaise, and prints the menu on
the place mat.

Harbor Haus, The

Copper Harbor. (906) 289–4502. B,L,D. $$
View of Lake Superior. German-American cooking,
plus whitefish and lake trout. Open May to
October.

Harvey Lo's Yummy House

1146 Wyandotte E., Windsor, Ontario.
(519) 252–1034. L,D. $$
A large menu that spans plum sauce in plastic
pouches to incredible mussels with black beans. Skip
the egg rolls; they appear to be commercial. The
specials are exciting. One of Windsor's oldest Chi-
nese eateries.   ☆ ☆

Hathaway House

U.S. 223 (w. 10 mi. from Exit 5), Blissfield.
(517) 486–2141. L,D. $$$
White Greek Revival house with a big heart for
American cooking. Claims to have one of the
longest-established salad bars and touts endless sup-
ply of prime rib. Friday nights only, there's a buffet
with crab, shrimp, and prime rib—all you can eat—
plus on Sunday a buffet of prime rib, baked ham,
fried chicken, and seafood. Accommodates large
groups.

Hattie's

111 St. Joseph, Suttons Bay. (616) 271–6222. D.
$$$
Succulent pheasant breast filled with a pecan stuff-
ing, complemented with an array of steamed vegeta-
bles, is typical of the upscale regional approach.
Chef Jim Milliman had good training, he ran the
kitchen at the Rowe Inn in Ellsworth for 3½ years
before opening Hattie's. Sesame-coated whitefish,
grilled tenderloin with fresh herbs, lobster medal-
lions in tequila lime butter sauce.   ☆ ☆ ☆ ☆

Hermann's European Cafe
214 N. Mitchell, Cadillac. (616) 775-9563. L,D. $$$
Lengthy menu with Continental veal, pasta, and
chicken dishes. Specialties are paper-thin wiener
schnitzel and apple strudel. New menu includes
Kansas City strip steak and Austrian-style beef
rouladen. Heart-healthy entrees available. Outstand-
ing desserts and ambitious wine list. Chef's deli
adjacent to restaurant. ☆ ☆ ☆

Hershel's Deli
*at Drury Inn, 585 W. Big Beaver (at I-75), Troy.
524-4770. B,L,D. $*
Neon reads "New York," but glitz is L.A. Fresh-
roasted turkey, fresh-ground coffee, fresh-squeezed
orange juice. Traditional deli items like cheese
blintzes, smoked fish, pickled tongue, hot brisket of
beef, and potato pancakes. Foyer houses complete
bakery. New York cheesecake is dense and divine.
Open 24 hours. ☆ ☆

Hillside
*41661 Plymouth (w. of Haggerty), Plymouth.
453-2002. L,D. Sun. Brunch. $$$*
"Bottom of the hill" dining room offers casual
soups, sandwiches, and chef's specials; "Top of the
Hill" is more fancy. Roulade of chicken with chorizo
sausage over tri-colored pasta; veal medallions in
marsala sauce; bourbon-marinated veal loin. Steaks
& chops. Six banquet rooms.

Himalaya
*841 Ouellette (at Elliott), Windsor, Ontario.
(519) 258-2804. D. $$*
Legendary Indian eatery with complement of French
food, too. The owner, simply known as "Oza," is a
former hotel chef educated in England who also
happens to be a health nut. He serves no red meat;
only chicken, seafood, and vegetables.

Historic Holly Hotel
*110 Battle Alley (at Broad St.), Holly. 634-5208.
L,D. $$$*
Vintage 19th century setting for up-to-date cuisine:
broiled whitefish with Hollandaise, poached Norwegian salmon in champagne sauce, and roast rack of
lamb. House wine is from nearby Seven Lakes Vine-
yard. Entertainment Thursday-Saturday in Comedy
Club. ☆ ☆

Hogan's

6450 Telegraph (at Maple), Birmingham. 626–1800.
L,D. $$
Bustling family tavern with broad menu ranging
from heart-healthy turkey salad to a mountainous
serving of nachos laced with spiced ground beef.
Chef Tom McGlone always has a surprise up his
sleeve: grilled buffalo burgers or a venison steak.
Also at 1555 E. Maple, Troy, 689–6300.   ☆ ☆

Home Sweet Home

43180 W. 9 Mile (E. of Novi Rd.), Novi. 347–0095.
L,D. $$
Black pillars and all, the old two-story mansion is
wrapped in homey kitsch and humor that carries
over to the menu: beef stew, meatloaf, chicken &
dumplings. Ribs are out of this world. So are the
brownies. (Wonder how many people have slid
down that banister?)   ☆ ☆

Homestead, The

M-22, 1 mi. n. of Glen Arbor. (616) 334–5000.
B,L,D. $$$
Non-guests need only obtain a pass at the office
desk for admittance to The Inn (make a reservation
in advance) or the Club Cafe. The Inn is the formal
restaurant (dinner only), with a Contemporary
American menu of pan-fried walleye, grilled sword-
fish and beef Wellington. Breakfast at the Club
Cafe, overlooking the beach, is the real treat.

Hotel Doherty

604 McEwan (at 5th St.), Clare. (517) 386–3441.
B,L,D. Sun. Brunch. $$
Since 1924, a traditional stop-off for travelers driv-
ing up north. Dining room is rimmed with murals of
four seasons in Michigan. Prime rib, broiled whitefish, stir-frys. Friday night seafood buffet. Sunday
brunch always features steamship round of beef and
chicken & dumplings.   ☆ ☆

Most entrees:		No stars	Not Rated
$	= less than $7	☆	Good
$$	= $7 to $13	☆ ☆	Very Good
$$$	= $13 to $19	☆ ☆ ☆	Excellent
$$$$	= $19 or more	☆ ☆ ☆ ☆	Outstanding
		☆ ☆ ☆ ☆ ☆	Superb
See p. xi for explanations.			

Hotel St. Regis

3071 W. Grand Blvd. (bet. Woodward & Cass),
Detroit. 873-3000. B,L,D. Sun. Brunch. $$$
Grand old duchess across from the General Motors
Building sports a new lobby, more banquet areas,
additional guest rooms, and—after three years—new
menus. Much improved cooking is still traditional—
mixed English grill, Dover sole, and whole Main
lobster at dinner; seafood salads, elaborate club
sandwich, chicken with porcini mushrooms at
lunch.   ☆ ☆ ☆

Houlihan's

adjacent to Somerset Mall, 2850 Coolidge Hwy.,
Troy. 649-2990. L,D. Sun. Brunch. $$
Singles tavern that's a cut above the pack. Lots of
Southwest dishes, some Cajun. Hottest seller is the
combination chicken-beef fajitas. Large menu of
appetizers, burgers, healthy stir-frys and salads, plus
London broil and barbecued baby back ribs. Dinners come with a miniature loaf of San Francisco
sourdough.   ☆ ☆ ☆

House of Ludington

223 Ludington (on the Bay), Escanaba.
(906) 786-4000. B,L,D. Sun. Brunch. $$$
Totally restored 1830s hotel with white linen dining
room. Veal Marsala, stuffed steak, homemade
pasta, chicken "Toren" (sauteed with shrimp, served
with asparagus over fettucine). Big attraction is five-
course sit-down Sunday brunch which draws fans
from as far away as Chicago.

Inn Season

500 E. Fourth (3 blks. e. of Main), Royal Oak.
547-7916. L,D. $$
Vegetarian menu, though fresh seafood is available.
Chalkboard specials range from gourmet whole
wheat pizza to fresh wild mushrooms sauteed with
garlic and sesame oil. Lots of Mexican vegetarian
dishes. East Indian fare featured on Thursday night.
No smoking.   ☆ ☆ ☆

Radicchio is not a rash. It's an Italian red leaf lettuce with
a pungent, sometimes bitter flavor.

Several downtown restaurants and bars offer complimen-
tary shuttle service to and from the theatres and Joe Lewis
arena. Call ahead.

Italian Cucina
39500 Ann Arbor Rd. (e. of I-275), Plymouth.
454–1444. L,D. $$
Italian cooking, but underneath it all, you detect
French training. Owner-chef Tim Coyne is another
"graduate" of the Golden Mushroom. Award-
winning minestrone, plus terrific shrimp-studded
fettucine alfredo. Almond-flavored cannoli and
exquisite tortes—all baked there. Fixed-price family-
style dinners on Sunday. ☆ ☆ ☆

Iva's
M-76 (Exit 195 off I-75), Sterling. (517) 654–3552.
L,D. $$
This chicken place off the highway is like Franken-
muth used to be. No rush, no lines, no obvious play
for tourists. Just an old frame house where honest
family-style chicken dinners have been famous for
more than 50 years. Chicken's cooked three ways;
Southern-fried is the best. Save room for pie. ☆ ☆

Ivanhoe Cafe
5249 Jos. Campau (3 blks. n. of Warren), Detroit.
925–5335. L,D. $$
Renowned for pan-fried perch and walleye lunches
Wednesday through Friday. Rest of the time, it's
ribs, corned beef, and kielbasa. Call ahead to check
hours—closed Saturday and Sunday. Nicknamed
"Polish Yacht Club" for charity-raising group that
meets there. ☆

Ivy's in the Park
Van Dyke Park Hotel and Conference Center, 31800
Van Dyke (bet. 13 & 14 Mile Rds.), Warren.
939–2860. B,L,D. Sun. Brunch. $$$
The target market is right across the street: the GM
Tech Center. Consequently, Ivy's promotes gray
flannel cuisine such as Oysters Rockefeller, tournedos of lotte, snails in puff pastry, plus mainstream
steaks, chops and stir-frys. Large Cruvinet. ☆

J.B.'s Bar & Grill
130 Seaway Rd., Sarnia, Ontario. (519) 332–0701.
D. $$
New sister restaurant to J.B.'s Harbor House. Lots
of appetizers, dance floor, disc jockey every night.
Children's menu available. Go early if you want a
quiet dinner.

J.B.'s Harbor House

485 Harbor Rd. (next to Centennial Park on Sarnia Bay), Sarnia, Ontario. (519) 332–0355. L,D. Sun. Brunch. $$

Boaters' haunt is just an anchor away from the marina. Known for 55-item salad bar. Steak, prime rib, seafood, and J.B.'s Mud Pie.

Jacoby's

624 Brush (Bet. E. Fort & Congress), Detroit. 962–7067. L,D. $

Detroit's oldest family saloon, specializing in reuben sandwiches and German specialties: knackwurst with kraut, potato pancakes, sauerbraten, and wiener schnitzel. Lawyers' hangout given its location opposite Wayne County Building.   ☆

Jacques Demers

in the Embassy Suites Hotel, 28100 Franklin Rd. (off Northwestern, s. of 12 Mile), Southfield. 355–2050. L,D. Sun. Brunch. $$$

Awfully fancy California-and Italian-style cooking for a sports lounge and restaurant decorated with hockey stuff. Admittedly, Jacques' special perch dish (sauteed), Jacques' special potatoes (Parisienne) and Jacques' special salad (not iceberg) score a hat trick. The Red Wings coach sits at the head table surrounded by ferns.   ☆ ☆ ☆

Jim's Tiffany Place & Greenhouse Cafe

116 E. Michigan (1 blk. e. of the Capitol), Lansing. (517) 372–4300. L,D. Sun. Brunch. $$$

Favorite of lawmakers and lobbyists; you can look out the front windows and see the State Capitol. Though it's the oldest restaurant in town (founded in 1914), it isn't showing many wrinkles. Continental cuisine with a splash of Greek. Prime rib, broiled salmon, Greek sampler called Pikilia, homemade honey wheat bread, and muffins. Sunday brunch.

Joe Bologna

in Wattles Square, 2135 17 Mile (at Dequindre), Sterling Heights. 939–5700. L,D. $

Flag-waving Italian dishes served with competence and family pride: homemade pasta, fennel-laced marinara sauce, Italian bread smothered with pesto, and deep-dish pizza that's major league. Excellent cannoli and chocolate cheesecake.   ☆ ☆

Joe Muer's Seafood

2000 Gratiot (at St. Aubin), Detroit. 567–1088. L,D. $$$$

Lives up to reputation as finest seafood spot in Detroit. Variety of two dozen sea and lake dwellers ranges from softshell crab and baby halibut to West Coast sturgeon. Steamed finnan haddie is a classic. One of the few fine dining establishments that doesn't take reservations for small groups and gets away with it. ☆ ☆ ☆

Joey's on Jefferson

7909 E. Jefferson (at Van Dyke), Detroit. 331–5450. L,D. $$$

Italian, with a big helping of glitz to lure the young and single. Beyond the dance floor, there's baked eggplant, fettucine Alfredo, and Joey's specialty— chicken sauteed in olive oil with garlic, potatoes, and artichoke hearts. ☆

Judy's Cafe

15714 W. Warren (2 1/2 blks. w. of Greenfield), Detroit. 581–8185. D. $

Five tables and short counter accommodate a couple dozen customers and real home-cooking, often ethnic. Personable owner-chef Judy Gardner dishes up friendly chatter as handily as split pea soup, beef stew with homemade biscuits, or garlic roast chicken. Save room for dessert. Breakfast and lunch on Saturday. ☆ ☆ ☆

Juilleret's

130 State, Harbor Springs. (616) 526–2821. B,L,D. $$

Ice cream and whitefish are stars at vintage family restaurant, purportedly the eatery that originated "planked" whitefish. It's baked on a hardwood platter and surrounded with piped mashed potatoes.
☆ ☆

Juilleret's

1418 Bridge (US 31 South), Charlevoix. (616) 547–9212. B,L,D. $

Forty-year-old family restaurant, recently sold by the Juilleret family, still specializes in same things it always did: cinnamon French toast for breakfast and whitefish at lunch and dinner. Homemade strawberry shortcake for dessert.

Justine

5010 Bay City Rd. (at US 10), Midland.
(517) 496-3012. L,D. $$$$

May be a long drive for dinner, but worth it. It's a
white-linen experience. Rabbit sausage with maple
sauce, oyster ragout with salmon caviar & buck-
wheat blini, fresh venison, grilled duck breast with
black currant sauce. Price of entree includes appetizer, intermezzo, salad, truffles, coffee, and dessert.
Adjoining Cafe Edward is more casual and moder-
ately priced. The menu is French bistro: veal head-
cheese and rillettes of pork; braised lamb shank with
lentils; smoked pork loin with "choucroute" potatoes. (Lunch not served in Justine.)   ☆ ☆ ☆ ☆

Kashmir

1139 University W. (at Wellington), Windsor,
Ontario. (519) 977-6173. L,D. $$

Unpretentious storefront throws on double layers of
table linen at night to dress up lengthy menu of
Indian dishes. Excellent soups, breads, biryanis,
tandoor-cooked meats, hot & sour Persian-style
curries with lentils. Shock! Most vegetables are
cooked al dente.   ☆ ☆ ☆

Kate's Kitchen

26558 W. Huron River Dr. (at Telegraph), Flat
Rock. 782-3909. B,L. $

Smell of cinnamon and apples are the big tip-off:
pie! You have, in fact, arrived at the temple of pie,
home-baked cinnamon rolls, bran muffins and
whole wheat bread. Fetching country dining room
specializes in breakfast—salt-cured ham and biscuits
included.   ☆ ☆

Kelly's Road House Cafe

14091 M-37 (on Old Mission Peninsula, 11 mi. out),
Traverse City. (616) 223-7200. L,D. $

Open beam ceiling and pine flooring create woodsy
atmosphere for smoked ribs, chicken, and duck.
Pretty interesting appetizers (smoked salmon spread,
fresh steamed artichoke), pastas (linguine with fresh
tomato, basil, and shrimp), and salads (grilled
chicken and smoked chef's) for a glorified bar. ☆ ☆

Kerrytown Bistro
in Kerrytown Market Place, 415 N. Fifth (at Kingsley), Ann Arbor. 994-6424. B,L,D. Sun. Brunch. $$
Handsome old brick cafe accented with modern art. French country cooking at dinner, but eclectic ethnic/American at lunch. Fabulous salt cod is pounded with olive oil and garlic for spreading on croutons; spicy sausage is baked in brioche, and beef shanks are braised in red wine. Menu changes every two months. Offbeat European wine list.

☆ ☆ ☆

Keweenaw Mountain Lodge
U.S. 41, Copper Harbor. (906) 289-4403. B,L,D. Sun. Brunch. $$
Complex includes log cottages, motel, and restaurant. Prime rib, lake trout. Saturday night smorgasbord. Open May to October.

Kingsley Inn
1475 N. Woodward (s. of Long Lake), Bloomfield Hills. 642-0100. B,L,D. $$$
Fifty-year-old institution attracts older, moneyed crowd. Lively coffee shop scene on weekends, bustling dining rooms and bar during the week. Food is American traditional but properly fussed over. Dover sole and prime rib. Breakfast in coffee shop only.

☆

Kola's Kitchen
in Indian Lanes Bowling Alley, 4500 13th St. (n. of Pennsylvania), Wyandotte. 283-4700. B,L. D—Friday only. $
A bowling alley dining room may sound like a weird entry in a restaurant guidebook, but so is the serving of muskrat. (In case you didn't know, it's a Downriver tradition.) Not to worry; by the time Johnny Kolakowski gets through sauteing one, it tastes like duck. He also creates unusual soups including reuben and Jamaican dolphin chowder. (Closed Saturday; Sunday—breakfast only.)

☆

Best wine buys on local restaurant lists are usually from Argentina, Chile, Spain, or Michigan.

Wise diners eat out on Tuesday night rather than Saturday. It's not as hectic.

Kruse and Muer

in Meadowbrook Mall, 60 N. Adams (at Walton), Rochester Hills. 375-2503. L,D. $$

Awesome pizza, delicious ribs, charbroiled chicken, fresh fish, and Charley's Chowder, and in the summertime truly delectable gazpacho. Daily pasta specials. You soon forget the plates are disposable and the tablecloths paper. Food's even more reasonable if you carry it out. Good place for families.

☆ ☆ ☆ ☆

La Becasse

intersection Cty. Rds. 616 and 675 (at e. end of Glen Lake), Burdickville. (616) 334-3944. D. $$$

The tangle of cars double-parked on the road remind you of the London Chop House on Saturday night. Business for new owners Peachy and John Rentenbach is booming. Elaborate American/French menu of Jeff Gabriel and Rob Welker changes weekly, but the style is oxtail consomme served inside a mushroom crepe, pinched cannelloni with a piquant vegetable filling (an entree), and deviled roast beef tenderloin marchand du vin. Reservations urged.

☆ ☆ ☆ ☆

La Cuisine

417 Pelissier, (first street after Ouellette), Windsor, Ontario. (519) 253-6432. L,D. $$

A French restaurant that doubles as a museum of French memorabilia. Owner-chef Francois Sully holds court in an open kitchen in the center of the dining room. Menu doesn't vary much: filet of pork with prunes and brandy sauce, bouillabaisse, and beef medallions with oyster mushrooms in Madeira sauce.

☆ ☆

La Familia

848 Woodward (n. of Square Lake), Pontiac. 338-8477. L,D. $

Famous for more than 25 years out N. Woodward for mountainous Nachos Supreme, Tostados Deluxe, guacamole, and margaritas by the liter. Sizes for all appetites make you promise you'll never order them elsewhere. Popular lunch spot. Regulars bring families evenings and weekends. At time of publication, scheduled to relocate.

La Fuente De Elena
3456 W. Vernor (at 24th), Detroit. 842–8277.
L,D. $
More personal than most Mexican spots thanks to
owner-chef Elena Gutierrez. She offers complimen-
tary soup (except in the summer) with the usual
taco-enchilada-chimichanga lineup.   ☆ ☆

La Notte
in Princeton Motel, 3032 Dougall (at E.C. Row
expressway), Windsor, Ontario. (519) 969-2750.
B,L,D. $$
Motel on such a commercial road is unlikely spot
for an Italian restaurant with upscale pretensions.
Menu and wine list are far-ranging. Shrimp with
white wine and garlic sauce, homemade gnocchi,
broiled pickerel filets, and the house specialty —
Scaloppine della Notte (thinly sliced veal with mush-
rooms in white wine sauce.   ☆ ☆ ☆

La Palette
Detroit Institute of Arts, 5200 Woodward (at Kirby),
Detroit. 833-1855. L. $$
Pretty as a picture. It's hard to believe there are
tablecloths, table service, and a nice little wine list in
a downtown museum. Daily seafood specials, sandwiches, entree salads, and a couple of fabulous
cakes.   ☆ ☆

La Rotisserie
Hyatt-Regency Dearborn, Fairlane Town Center,
Dearborn. 593-1234. D. $$$$
Luxury dining room is on the mend after starting
out with such a bang in 1976, then falling to embar-
rassing depths. New-style American cooking has
featured sea scallop carpaccio, grilled quail with
sweetbreads, Coleman beef, and intricate desserts
such as chocolate creme caramel with fresh raspber-
ries. Pianist adds to the already intimate air.
                                            ☆ ☆ ☆ ☆

La Shish
12918 Michigan Ave. (e. of Schaefer), Dearborn.
584-4477. L,D. $$
Juice bar makes this new Lebanese spot extra invit-
ing. A full menu of salads, dips, and lamb &
chicken specialties, but keep your eye on what the
neighborhood customers order — shawarma and a
mug of fresh-squeezed carrot juice.   ☆ ☆

Laikon Cafe
569 Monroe (bet. Beaubien & St. Antoine), Detroit.
963-7058. L,D. $$
Beyond the typical Greek dishes are specialties such
as broiled seabass with endive greens and "candy
custard" for dessert. A comfortable dining room
with popular balcony seating. Complete list of
Greek wines. ☆ ☆

Lansdowne
201 W. Atwater (at Civic Center Dr., behind Cobo
Hall), Detroit. 259-6801.
Detroit's only permanently floating restaurant. (At
time of publication, closed for remodeling.)

Lark, The
6430 Farmington Rd. (at Maple), West Bloomfield.
661-4466. D. $$$$
Portuguese country inn dressed in attractive tilework
and leather is the epitome of luxury dining. Entree
price includes splendid hors d'oeuvre cart, choice of
second course, salad, and sorbet. Specialties are
shellfish and sausage cooked in copper cataplana
pots and rack of lamb Genghis Khan. Desserts are
extra, but worth it, especially Salzburger Nockerl.
Jim and Mary Lark are on-premise owners who see
to every detail. Outstanding service and au courant
wine list. Chef is Marcus Haight. ☆ ☆ ☆ ☆ ☆

Las Brisas
8445 W. Vernor (at Springwell), Detroit. 842-8252.
L,D. $$
Weekends come alive with mariachi music, but the
rest of the time, the action is on the plate: all the
Mexican predictables plus pork and hominy soup,
tripe soup, goat or lamb bathed in molé, and a
number of taco dishes served with pico de gallo (a
fresh tomato salsa spiked with cilantro). ☆

Le Metro
in Applegate Square, 29855 Northwestern Hwy. (at
Inkster), Southfield. 353-2757. L,D. $$$
Eclectic French-bistro cooking reminiscent of old
Money Tree days. Noon menu includes ratatouille,
"stock pot lunch," and chicken strudel; at dinner,
braised short ribs over brown rice and black beans,
steamed halibut, and medallions of veal stuffed with
boursin cheese and sun-dried tomatoes. ☆ ☆ ☆ ☆

Le Peep

in the Woodward Square, 355 S. Woodward (s. of Maple), Birmingham. 258-9678. B,L. Sun. Brunch. $
For breakfast addicts. Homespun pancakes, french toast, omelets and frittatas are served every day until 2:30 p.m. Best known for "pan-handled dishes and pampered eggs" — skillet dishes with basted eggs perched on mounds of potatoes, cheese, and sausage. Also at 455 E. Eisenhower, at State St., Ann Arbor, 662-2272; 33010 Northwestern Hwy. at 14 Mile Rd., West Bloomfield, 851-6678; and 21200 Haggerty, across from Novi Hilton, Novi, scheduled to open in late '89.   ☆

Leelanau Country Inn

149 E. Harbor Hwy. (M-22, 8 mi. s. of Leland), Maple City. (616) 228-5060. D. Sun. Brunch. $$
Ex-Chuck Muer manager John Sisson uses many of his former employer's ideas in an old country house turned restaurant. Farm antiques create warm, cozy ambiance for escargots in casino butter, seafood alfredo, whitefish, pork Wellington, and prime rib. Leelanau County wines by the glass.   ☆ ☆ ☆

Left Field Deli

1266 Michigan (e. of Tiger Stadium), Detroit. 961-7968. B,L. $
Owner Max Silk entertains everybody from priests and judges to humble folk who simply need an ear to listen. Soups, sandwiches, and salads are as nourishing as Silk's benevolent approach to people.   ☆

Legs Inn

Scenic Hwy. M119 (bet. Harbor Springs & Mackinaw City), Cross Village. (616) 526-2281. L,D. $$
A sight to see: Literally a pile of Michigan fieldstones made into a bar-restaurant that celebrates a unique blend of Polish and Indian cultures. Furniture is constructed entirely of twisted tree roots, stumps, and driftwood. New owners have not only cleaned up the place, but the once-tarnished reputation. Smoked whitefish, sandwiches, soups, Polish combination plates, plus 60 beers from around the world.   ☆

Lelli's

7618 Woodward (at Bethune), Detroit. 871–1590.
L,D. $$$

One of the cornerstones of Italian dining in Detroit.
Though impatient career waiters love to order for
you, just make it clear you want the minestrone and
the famous filet mignon or Shrimp Lelli. If the
espresso machine is out of order again, try asking
another passing server—your luck could change and
it's worth the challenge.   ☆ ☆ ☆

Lepanto

316 S. Main (s. of 11 Mile), Royal Oak. 541–2228.
L,D. $$

"New" Italian country food in smart mauve setting.
Husband/wife team Chris and Laura Claire keep the
menu as light and original as possible. Bagna cauda
(anchovied dipping sauce), rosemary-scented focaccia
(flatbread), fabulous lasagna built of paper-thin
pasta and flavored with prosciutto, plus cannoli
stuffed with white chocolate mousse.   ☆ ☆ ☆

Les Auteurs

in Washington Square Plaza, 222 Sherman Dr. (just
n. of Fourth & Washington), Royal Oak. 544–2887.
L,D. $$

Crayons, butcher paper, and willowy herbed bread-
sticks mark a restaurant that isn't like the rest. Chef
Keith Famie goes hip and haute with everything
from spicy chicken and buffalo chili topped with
fried polenta to skewered shrimps and scallops in
plum sauce. Barbecued chicken, designer pizza,
sassy pastas, and—if they're in season—truffles.
Dieting? Then feast on all the pretty people.

☆ ☆ ☆ ☆

Lim's Garden

22295 Michigan Ave. (e. of Military), Dearborn.
563-4393. L,D. $$

New, expanded blue dining room breaks out of
former red and black mold. Owners Buckmon and
Connie Woo and family lend personal touch. Mon-
golian beef, Szechuan shrimp, cashew chicken. Sup-
plies half of Dearborn with carryouts. (Open daily
till 3 a.m. for dinner.)   ☆ ☆ ☆

Lindell A.C.

1310 Cass (at Michigan), Detroit. 964–1122. L,D. $
Detroit's first true sports bar, where stars really do hang out. Owners John and Jimmy Butsicaris treat everybody—jocks and fans alike—as if they were family. "We get involved," said John. Menu never changes: hamburger, cheeseburger, steak sandwich, grilled cheese & fries. ☆

Lindos Taverna

511 Monroe (bet. Brush & Beaubien), Detroit. 961–2070. L,D. $$
One of the newer additions to Greektown. Beyond the touristy predictables are more contemporary Greek dishes such as grilled chicken breast with jumbo shrimp in lemon-butter sauce, sauteed chicken strips with mushrooms and green pepper over rice, plus calamari and mussels. ☆ ☆

Little Harry's Restaurant

2681 E. Jefferson (bet. Chene & Jos. Campau), Detroit. 259–2636. L,D. $$$
Vintage supper club atmosphere with vintage supper-club menu: charbroiled filet mignon, Veal Oscar, Beef Wellington, and broiled pickerel. But who needs food? Catch the drinks and action around the piano bar. Sequins recommended; Grecian Formula obligatory. ☆

Little River Cafe

715 S. Kalamazoo (Exit 60 off I-94), Paw Paw. (616) 657–6035. L,D. $$
Wine country atmosphere decorated with enlarged artist's renderings of Michigan wine labels. Not surprising, there is a lengthy Michigan wine list to match the broiled whitefish, pan-fried pickerel, and cranberry-glazed duck. ☆ ☆

Loaf and Mug

236 Culver (bet. Butler & Griffith), Saugatuck. (616) 857–2974. L,D. Sun. Brunch. $
Casual name for a serious deli that offers premium kosher meats, organically grown vegetables when possible, and doesn't own a grill or deep-fryer. About 15 deli sandwiches plus salads, quiche, and soups. Attached bakery cranks out muffins and croissants. Michigan wines are featured. ☆ ☆

London Chop House

155 W. Congress (bet. Shelby & Griswold), Detroit. 962-0277. L,D. $$$$

New owners have restored old glow. Downtown's venerable luxury eatery has been totally redecorated, yet still feels much the same. Cuts a wide swath when it comes to creative American cooking, and service. Noted dishes are lobster bisque, mess of perch, and most recently, salmon "osso bucco." Award-winning wine list, late kitchen on weekends, and dancing make this restaurant unique. Dress to kill. ☆ ☆ ☆ ☆

Long Branch Restaurant

595 N. Lapeer (10 mi. n. of The Palace of Auburn Hills), Oxford. 628-6500. L,D. Sun. Brunch. $$

Western-theme with broad menu that runs from prime rib to half-pound burgers. Homemade rolls, buns, and desserts. All-you-can-eat battered perch for $11.95. Comedy Club on Thurs.-Sat.

Lord Fox

5400 Plymouth (off M-14 bet. U.S. 23 & Ford Rd.), Dixboro. 662-1647. L,D. $$

Don't be misled by casualness of lipstick-red table-cloths, a fieldstone fireplace and knotty pine paneling. Rural Washtenaw Cty. restaurant gives new meaning to roadhouse food — N.Y. strip with char-grilled onions, slow-roasted prime rib au jus, and grilled Indiana chicken breast with mushroom-Chardonnay sauce. Excellent wine list. ☆ ☆ ☆

Lorien

406 Bay (in Gaslight Plaza), Petoskey. (616) 347-4434. L. $

A plain pink room that serves only lunch. But what a lunch. Just simple pastas, salads, muffins, soups, and pies, but you won't find better anywhere up north. Owners David and Sheila Rowlison are ex-truck drivers who love to cook, but they never had a day of classes in their life. Problem is, they much prefer the private catering of desserts. Let's just pray they keep the restaurant going. ☆ ☆ ☆ ☆

Louie Linguini's Ristorante
139 Ouellette (at Pitt, 1 blk. from river), Windsor,
Ontario. (519) 252-6969. D. $$$
Owners Kathy and Paul Borrelli have dropped lunch
and swung into a more serious mode since opening
three years ago. Where the menu used to be mostly
pasta, it now carries close to 10 meat entrees includ-
ing a veal chop stuffed with shrimp and basil,
broiled lamb chops with wild mushroom sauce, and
jumbo shrimp in white wine on angel hair pasta.
Bracing "long" espresso prepares you for flight of
steps back up to street level.

Louisiana Creole Gumbo
2051 Gratiot (at St. Aubin), Detroit. 446-9639.
L,D. $
Classic creole carryout spot: spicy seafood gumbo,
red beans and rice, shrimp creole, jambalaya, and
crumbly corn bread muffins. Save room for peach
cobbler and sweet potato pie. Dining room and
carryout at 17171 Livernois, at McNichols, Detroit,
861-4310.   ☆ ☆

Lucky Kitchen Restaurant
754 Ouellette (at Wyandotte), Windsor, Ontario.
(519) 253-7255. L,D. $$
Good luck, if you're the indecisive sort: menu of
Hong Kong and Szechuan dishes is as long as the
New York phone directory. Not to worry, Confucius
say: Close eyes and point. Quality is usually superb.
Seafood is always fresh, vegetables cooked to al
dente perfection. Dim sum served daily from 11-3.

☆ ☆

Macardy's
15750 Hall Rd. (e. of Hayes), Mt. Clemens.
263-5001. L,D. $$
Large dining room with equally large menu but not
just another polyester palace. Prime rib, lamb
chops, scads of fresh seafood, homemade pasta,
fresh-baked rolls brushed with basil butter, and even
an occasional special of duck breast with raspberry
sauce. A boon for Macomb business types seeking
"safe" sophisticated fare.   ☆ ☆ ☆

Machus Red Fox

6676 Telegraph (at Maple), Birmingham. 626–4200.
L,D. $$$$
Pretentious Continental dining overseen by chef
Leopold Schaeli. Though many people remember
this restaurant as the last spot Jimmy Hoffa was
seen alive, they also talk about the rack of lamb,
chateaubriand, and broiled Dover sole. Impeccable
service. Extensive wine list.   ☆ ☆

Machus Sly Fox

725 S. Hunter (s. of Maple), Birmingham. 642–6900.
L,D. Sun. Brunch. $$$
Traditional American fine dining. Specialty is roast
prime rib, but there are plenty of lighter chicken and
seafood dishes. Machus salad with the chilled fork is
customary, along with assorted pastries such as Chef
Leopold's triple chocolate mousse torte and lemon
crunch cake.   ☆ ☆

Mackinnon's

126 E. Main (bet. 7 & 8 Mile), Northville. 348–1991.
L,D. $$$
Lace curtains and dozens of wild game paintings
create cozy homespun Michigan feel. Foodwise,
owner-chef Tom Mackinnon carries out same theme
with wild turkey tenderloin, house-smoked salmon,
and a Scotch grill of duck, lamb, and salmon. Lots
of creativity, plus dynamic wine list.   ☆ ☆ ☆

Mackinnon's Macomb Inn

45199 Cass (n. of Hall Rd.), Utica. 726–0770. L,D.
$$
Tom Mackinnon's redo of the former Darby's.
Homey, family-oriented eatery abounds with
surprises—i.e., the serving of bread with not only
butter but a whole baked clove of garlic, duck
mousse, and tapenade. Duck with raspberry sauce,
house-smoked whitefish, veal, pork.

Magnolia Grille on the Idler Riverboat, The

515 Williams (in Old Harbor Village), South Haven.
(616) 637-8435. L,D. $$$
Cajun and Caribbean aromas permeate the lower-
deck dining room of docked antique Mississippi
riverboat. Blackened prime rib with barbecued
shrimp over Cajun pasta; marinated filet mignon
seared with Caribbean spices. Signature dish is coconut shrimp. Nightly fish specials.   ☆ ☆

Marco's Dining & Cocktails
in Village Commons, 32758 Grand River (e. of Farmington Rd.), Farmington. 477-7777. L,D. $$
Most definitely, a new and contemporary style for the Conte family, owners of the former Rina's of Detroit eatery. Total Italian menu with fresh made pastas, stuffed chicken, veal chops, and steaks. Unlike Rina's, no pizza.

Maria's Pizzeria
19220 Grand River (1/2 mi. w. of Southfield Expressway), Detroit. 533-2910. L,D. $$
Popular neighborhood Italian haunt, complete with chianti bottles, red checkered tablecloths, and dynamite pizza. Also veal and pasta. Don't miss the garlic bread.

Mariner North, The
226 Gratiot (on U.S. 41), Copper Harbor. (906) 289-4637. L,D. $$
Travelers' complex includes motel, gift shop, restaurant, and lounge. Mostly seafood — trout and whitefish.

Mario's
4222 Second (bet. Willis & Canfield), Detroit. 833-9425. L,D. $$
Brusque, efficient waiters administer Italian menu as complete as a Sears catalog. Heavy-duty meals come with antipasto, salad, soup, the main course and more. Known for veal.   ☆ ☆

Mary Ann's Kitchen
2711 N. Woodward (s. of Square Lake), Bloomfield Hills. 332-0088. B,L,D. $
Cafe/carryout does great job with breakfast: tempting bran muffins, gooey pecan rolls, cheese-swollen omelets and robust coffee. Rest of the day, it's a chic neighborhood deli with salads, sandwiches, and simple entrees. Short dinner menu features spectacular tortellini primavera. Also at 100 W. Big Beaver (at Livernois) in Liberty Center, 680-1866. Troy closed Sat. & Sun. Bloomfield closed Sun.   ☆ ☆

Mason-Girardot Alan Manor, The

3203 Peter St. (at Mill), Windsor, Ontario.
(519) 253-9212. D. $$$

Interesting Turkish and Continental cooking doubles charm of this historic house west of the Ambassador Bridge. Dining rooms are furnished with hundred-year-old British antiques. Turkish specialties include boerek (a savory pie of cheese and herbs), the memorable stuffed eggplant appetizer called Imam Bay-ildi, and kebabs of lamb and seasoned ground beef. Fixed-price Turkish feast daily.   ☆ ☆ ☆

Maude's

314 S. Fourth (bet. Liberty & Williams), Ann Arbor.
662-8485. L,D. $$

A favorite of downtown office workers. Contemporary menu of grilled chicken with artichokes in Bearnaise, chargrilled salmon, and an eclectic mixed grill of swordfish, chicken, and sausage. Specialty is slow-roasted baby back ribs. With all this "now" food, the decor is Victorian.   ☆ ☆

Mayflower Hotel

827 W. Ann Arbor Trail (at Main), Plymouth.
453-1620. B,L,D. Sun. Brunch. $$

Steeped in pilgrim history though traditional Thanksgiving feast has been limited to groups of 50 or more. (Notice the last four digits of the telephone number?) The Mayflower Room and the Steak House offer steamed Norwegian scrod, steaks, ribs, and chicken. Round Table Club is fine dining for members only.

McNally's Delicatessen

1300 Porter (at Brooklyn), Detroit. 963-8833.
B,L. $

Name and neighborhood may be Irish, but the flavors are Jewish: hearty rye bread, corned beef and pastrami, broccoli-potato soup thick enough to eat with a fork, and giant oatmeal cookies with date and raspberry fillings. Original tin ceiling, hardwood floor, soda fountain chairs and vintage city photographs are a break from usual sea of Formica. Practically in the shadow of Tiger Stadium.   ☆ ☆

Medallion
in Crosswinds Mall, 4343 Orchard Lake (at Lone Pine), West Bloomfield. 851-5540. L,D. $$$
Hidden oasis at far end of the mall. Ex-Money Tree chef Eddie Matteson churns out signature medallions of beef tenderloin in Bearnaise sauce, salmon steamed in white wine, grilled chicken on tri-colored pasta, and whitefish with oyster mushrooms. ☆ ☆ ☆

Meritage, The
6880 E. 12 Mile (bet. Van Dyke & Mound), Warren. 573-4470. L,D. Sun. Brunch. $$$
Jeff Baldwin, former chef of The Whitney, and the three Palshauj brothers transformed the old Schmid Haus into a handsome, contemporary restaurant of trendy proportions not seen on the northeast side. Walleye pike coated in toasted hazelnuts, "beggar's purses" of brie and mango chutney, outstanding soups, gourmet pizza, and grilled lamb chops stuffed with garlic, basil, and spinach. What a deal: Whitney quality; Warren prices. ☆ ☆ ☆

Metropolitan Musicafe
in Washington Square Plaza, 326 W. Fourth (at S. Lafayette), Royal Oak. 542-1990. L,D. $$
Dance club that tries to outrock the Hard Rock. Steaks, stir-frys, and sandwiches are secondary to the pink Cadillac over the bar, dress from Madonna, and scores of celebrity guitars and gold records. ☆

Mexican Fiesta
24310 Ford Rd. (w. of Telegraph), Dearborn. 274-3066. L,D. $
Popular family restaurant that's cranked out homemade chorizo and refried beans for more than 25 years. Snappy service, down-to-earth prices, huge portions. Don't expect to finish burritos if you order guacamole first. Also at 44401 Ford Rd., at Sheldon, Canton, 981-1048. ☆ ☆

Mexican Town
3457 Bagley (at 24th), Detroit. 841-5811. L,D. $
Modern tavern setting attracts families more than young singles. Seafood and steak in addition to the required Mexican nibbles. ☆ ☆

Mexican Village

2600 Bagley (at 18th), Detroit. 237-0333. L,D. $
This is the oldest Mexican eatery in the area. Especially noted for the "Arizonian" plate—a combination platter with a taste of everything: salad, taco, burrito, enchilada, chimichanga, and rice & beans. Also at 47350 Van Dyke, n. of 21 Mile, in Utica, 254-2290. ☆ ☆

Michael's

in The Corner's Shopping Plaza, 17600 W. 13 Mile (at Southfield), Birmingham. 540-4444. L,D. Sun. Brunch. $$
Awesomely stylish for being in a mall. Bi-coastal menu: miniature pizzas, vegetable strudel, stir-fried wild mushrooms. Main courses include mixed grill, baby back ribs, and hazelnut-coated walleye. Sixteen wines by the glass. Piano bar Wednesday-Saturday. ☆ ☆

Midtown Cafe

139 S. Woodward (s. of Maple), Birmingham. 642-1133. L,D. Sun. Brunch. $$$
Still the trendiest bar scene in Oakland Cty. But, occasionally, people do nibble. Grilled chicken salad with mixed greens, fettuccine with salmon, sauteed Dover sole, and fresh fruit desserts. Kitchen's open daily until 1:30 a.m. ☆ ☆

Miki

106 S. First (at Huron), Ann Arbor. 665-8226. L,D. $$
Stark black and white decor matches simplicity of raw fish with vinegared rice or thinly sliced beef poached in broth. Sushi bar is bossed by co-owner Taka Nagaie who puts on quite a show. Save room for unusually flavored ice creams: green tea, ginger, ogura, and plum wine. ☆ ☆ ☆

Miller's Country House

16409 Red Arrow Hwy. (3 mi. n. of New Buffalo), Union Pier. (616) 469-5950. L,D. $$$
Two main dining rooms overlook gardens. Upscale California-style menu and display kitchen. Roasted garlic with chevre, cioppino, Norwegian salmon in cucumber-dill sauce, chargrilled rack of lamb, flourless chocolate cake.

Mini Restaurant, The

475 University W. (4 blks. w. of Ouellette), Windsor, Ontario. (519) 254-2221. L,D. $

Not diminutive when it comes to the size of the menu. Owner Tony Lam, sole cook, turns out scores of noodle dishes, curries, and marvelous barbecued beef. El cheapo and fresh. ☆ ☆

Mitch's Tavern

4000 Cass Elizabeth Rd. (at Cass Lake Rd.), Pontiac. 682-1616. L,D. $$

Popular family spot that's always crowded no matter when you arrive. Known for ribs, Greek salad, pizza, and breadsticks. ☆ ☆

Mon Jin Lau

1515 E. Maple (at Stephenson Hwy.), Troy. 689-2332. L,D. $$

Sophisticated Asian/Chinese setting to sip Chardonnay with softshell crab or Sauvignon Blanc with spring rolls. Favorites are Thai chicken with broccoli and onions on spicy peanut sauce; whole steamed pickerel with ginger and garlic; and crispy Dover sole with shiitake mushrooms. ☆ ☆

Monchelle Lamoure

149 Pierce (s. of Maple), Birmingham. 647-4140. L. $$

Elegant little cafe does a fair lunch and decent afternoon tea, but, oh, that counter of chocolate candy! Twelve flavors of truffles and pralines add up to a dozen ways to drive you crazy, or at least to the nearest Weight Watchers' class. High tea on Thursday evening. ☆

Money Tree, The

333 Fort (at Washington Blvd.), Detroit. 961-2445. L,D. $$$

Innovative French/American cooking, interesting wines and one of the best dessert trays in town. Chef Tom Foydel's experience at New York's Le Cirque shows in his perfectly roasted venison with polenta, or tuna steak still pale pink in the center. Save room for pitch-black pecan pie and heavenly dense cheesecake. Popular lunch spot. Bar is Yuppie hangout. ☆ ☆ ☆ ☆

Montague Inn

1581 S. Washington (bet. M-46 & Holland),
Saginaw. (517) 752-3939. L,D. $$$
Intimate dining in restored English-style mansion.
Menu changes every three months. Chicken with
fresh fruit salsa, stuffed turbot, Norwegian salmon
in strawberry-wine sauce. Known for hazelnut
cheesecake.

Moro's

6535 Allen Rd. (at Southfield Rd.), Allen Park.
382-7152. L,D. $$
Even Bloomfield diners trek Downriver to this spot.
Unpretentious atmosphere combined with slightly
pretentious international menu. Sliced tenderloin in
espagnole sauce, veal piccante, veal marsala, Hungarian paprikash, and Greek saganaki. Specials run
from scampi to lobster. ☆ ☆ ☆

Moveable Feast, The

326 W. Liberty (at Second), Ann Arbor. 663-3278.
L,D. $$$$
Old Victorian house sticks to classic French cooking
with injections of American regional flair. Seasonal
menu with items such as braised Maine lobster with
caviar cream; medallions of beef tenderloin, hunter-
style; turban of Michigan rainbow trout with shrimp
mousseline. Breads and desserts are specialties.
Good spot to impress a date. A la carte or fixed-
price menu. ☆ ☆ ☆

Mr. B's

M-28, Munising. (906) 387-3872. B,L,D. $
Daily all-you-can-eat buffet with changing themes:
Mexican, pizza & ribs, and seafood. Always 10
salads and pudding for dessert.

Mr. Paul's Chop House

29850 Groesbeck (n. of 12 Mile), Roseville.
777-7770. L,D. $$$
White tablecloth oasis in desert of tool and die
shops. Formal service, tableside cooking, decent
wine list. Specialties include Caesar salad, veal,
steaks, seafood. ☆ ☆

Muchachos

12601 Gratiot (near Whittier), Detroit. 521-7260.
L,D. $$
South-of-the border remake of former Little Cafe.
Clean and cheery. Spicy salsa, hot tortilla chips and
a dandy combination plate. Monstrous Margaritas
need two hands to steady.   ☆ ☆

Murdock's

in Crooks Corners, 2086 Crooks (n. of M-59),
Rochester Hills. 852-0550. L,D. $$
Live jazz and a bustling bar with one of the longest
beer lists in the state. Chaldean owners may emphasize mammoth hamburgers, light chicken and seafood dishes, but unacclaimed specialties are falafel,
tabbouleh, baba ghanouge and hommous.   ☆ ☆

Musashi

2000 Town Center (10 1/2 Mile & Evergreen),
Southfield. 358-1911. L,D. $$$
Sushi outpost in the Prudential Town Center. A
favorite of area businessmen, not all of whom are
Japanese. Sashimi, tempura, teriyaki, and nabe-
mono dinners. Tatami rooms available.

Natraj

26799 Greenfield (s. of 11 Mile), Southfield.
557-7070. L,D. $$$
An upscale Indian setting matched by thick, gutsy
curries, soups that sing with cilantro, and moist
tandoori-grilled meats. Mixed grill offers taste of
everything. Indian buffet at lunch is a little pricey,
but worth it. Saturday — dinner only.   ☆ ☆ ☆

Nelson's Summer Place

U.S. 41 (5 mi. s. of Houghton), Chassell.
(906) 523-4848. D. $$
Enclosed glass porch overlooks Portage Lake. Prime
rib, marinated steak, charbroiled shrimp on a
skewer. Main course includes relish plate, soup,
salad, vegetable and homemade bread.

New Hellas

583 Monroe (at St. Antoine), Detroit. 961-5544.
L,D. $$

Old-time Greek eatery (since 1901) where soups, especially lentil, are classics. Many broiler items— veal, lamb chops, chicken, lamb kebabs, and New York strips. Most extensive wine inventory in Greektown, but you have to request the captain's list. ☆ ☆

Nicky's

concourse level Top of Troy building, 755 W. Big Beaver (at I-75), Troy. 362-1262. L,D. $$$

It may be elbow-room only at the sprawling bar but the dining scene is equally alive. Great London broil at lunch; Provimi veal and seafood at dinner. Crowd is over 35 and graying at the temples. ☆ ☆ ☆

Niki's Pizzeria

735 Beaubien (at Lafayette), Detroit. 961-4303.
L,D. $

Pizzaphiles call it the best there is downtown. New additions to menu include chicken kebabs, lamb chops, and a Greek combination plate. Popular outdoor cafe in summer. Taverna upstairs adds tablecloths and a view. Also at 1203 Washington Blvd. at State, Detroit, 963-8160; and 1101 Michigan Ave. at Washington Blvd., Detroit, 961-9333. ☆ ☆

1913 Room, The

Amway Grand Plaza Hotel, 187 Pearl (at Monroe), Grand Rapids. (616) 774-2000. L,D. Sun. Brunch. $$$

Precision contemporary American cooking is steeped in old-world elegance—luxurious booths, chandeliers, mirrored columns, and acres of lustrous wood. Appetizers include unique packages of escargot bundled in crisp pastry and baked seafood ravioli in chervil cream; main courses run from grilled salmon in avocado butter to marvelous scaloppini of veal with a nest of fettucine alfredo. ☆ ☆ ☆ ☆

Q—Who has the best gazpacho in town? A—Kruse and Muer in Rochester Hills.

Prix fixe refers to a multi-course meal with one flat price. Sometimes dessert is extra. Drinks and the tip always are.

1940 Chop House
1940 E. Jefferson (at St. Aubin), Detroit. 567–1940.
L,D. $$$
Baubles and beads are required dress; neon glitz
attracts a dressy crowd. A glorified steakhouse, but
there's also a selection of lamb, chicken, and sea-
food. Additional bonus is bargain approach to good
Burgundy wines and cognac; they're priced to flow
like water. Entertainment.   ☆ ☆ ☆

Nipponkai
511 W. 14 Mile (bet. Crooks & Livernois), Clawson.
288-3210. L,D. $$$
Loyal American following usually outnumbers the
Japanese. At tableside, specialties are tempura, teri-
yaki, and one-pot dishes called nabemono (for two
or more). Delicious broiled eel. Also at 32443
Northwestern Hwy., bet. Orchard Lake & Middlebelt, Farmington Hills, 737-7220.   ☆ ☆ ☆

Norm's Oyster Bar & Grill
29110 Franklin Rd. (at Northwestern Hwy.),
Southfield. 357-4442. L,D. $$
Raw bar may be gone, but not the seafood. There
are five fish specials daily plus oysters on the half
shell. Specialties are sauteed perch, raspberry
chicken over fettucine, and lemon chicken fettucine.
A mecca for local doctors and business people. ☆ ☆

Norman's Eton Street Station
245 S. Eton (at Maple), Birmingham. 647-7774.
L,D. Sun. Brunch. $$
Young professionals mingle at giant oval bar
beneath vaulted roof of old Birmingham train station. Though the scene almost makes the food sec-
ondary, nobody knocks the seafood, lasagna, ribs,
sticky chicken, and thick burgers. Variety of wines
by the glass.   ☆ ☆

Normandie on the Park
6525 Second (at W. Grand Blvd.), Detroit.
871-5523. L,D. $$$
GM's other meeting room. Mostly blue-suiters at
lunch. Tons of beef, booze, smoke, and loud chat-
ter. Roadhouse menu features chopped sirloin,
steaks, calves' liver with bacon and onions, shrimp,
and scallops. Popular after-theatre spot.   ☆ ☆

Northwoods Supper Club, The
260 Northwoods Rd. (off US 41), Marquette.
(906) 228-4343. L,D. Sun. Brunch. $$$
Family and special occasion restaurant that's been a
dining legend for 50 years. Located in a log building
in the woods, specialties are broiled fish, prime rib,
tournedos of beef, chicken Oscar. Smorgasbord on
Tuesdays. Seafood buffet on Fridays. Three salad
bars.

Oakley's
161 E. Michigan (at Portage), Kalamazoo.
(616) 349-6436. L,D. $$$$
Little is left of atrium eatery's casual past; nightly
specials show the serious intentions of chef Chip
Marbach, formerly of Le Francais (Wheeling, IL).
Medallions of veal with morel cream sauce, roast
duckling of the day, fresh fish and wild game. Wine
list is serious, too.

Old Country Haus
U.S. 41 (n. of Calumet), Kearsarge. (906) 337-4626.
B,L,D. $$
Log cabin eatery with German-American menu,
including lake fish. Same owner operates The Harbor Haus in Copper Harbor. Open year-round.

Old German
120 W. Washington (at Ashley), Ann Arbor.
662-0737. L,D. $$
Such an institution that loyal customers now span
two generations. A fire in 1975 put it out of busi-
ness for two years, but owner Bud Metzger and
passionate patrons wouldn't let it die. Menu comple-
ments extensive collection of beer steins. Sauerbra-
ten, wiener schnitzel, spareribs and kraut, German
meat patties, plus sides of spatzen (noodles), rotkohl
(red cabbage), and homemade German potato salad,
cucumber salad, and applesauce.   ☆ ☆

Most entrees:		No stars	Not Rated
$	= less than $7	☆	Good
$$	= $7 to $13	☆ ☆	Very Good
$$$	= $13 to $19	☆ ☆ ☆	Excellent
$$$$	= $19 or more	☆ ☆ ☆ ☆	Outstanding
		☆ ☆ ☆ ☆ ☆	Superb
See p. xi for explanations.			

Old Parthenon

579 Monroe (at St. Antoine), Detroit. 961-5111.
L,D. $$

Cherished Greektown eatery with notable dishes like the "special Greek salad" (big enough to be an appetizer platter) and the Parthenon cake topped with owner Tommy Peristeris' mom's recipe for pineapple and whipped cream custard. Fresh green beans & lamb every day. At time of publication, Peristeris was opening the "New Parthenon" five doors away at 547 Monroe.   ☆ ☆

Olde Country Steak House

1717 London Rd. (s. of 402 Hwy.), Sarnia, Ontario.
(519) 542-7171 or (519) 542-7161. L,D. Sun.
Brunch. $$$

Old English atmosphere has been newly updated. Buffet six nights a week, plus hot lunch buffet, and Sunday brunch. Prime rib, seafood, chicken. Accommodates large groups.

Olde Town Cafe

7636 Auburn Rd. (bet. Van Dyke & Mound), Utica.
739-2090. L,D. $$

A local haunt for everybody from Utica farmers to doctors at Troy's Beaumont Hospital. Regulars consider it a simple, unpretentious place where the portions and price are right. Fast service with a "honey" or "darling" thrown in for free. Steak sandwich, fried fish, shrimp, burgers, and heaping salads. So dark you need a flashlight.   ☆

Oliverio's

3832 N. Woodward (1 blk. s. of Normandy), Royal
Oak. 549-3344. L,D. $$$

This Italian food is so New York in style, you think you're really on Mulberry Street. And that's exactly what Brooklyn-raised Artie Oliverio, chef and owner, had in mind. Eggplant sorentino, spiedini alla romano, pumpkin tortelloni, and a variety of veal and seafood dishes. A smart place to be seen.   ☆ ☆ ☆ ☆

The term "American bistro" has little to do with its French counterpart, except the atmosphere is casual and prices moderate.

Radicchio is not a rash. It's an Italian red leaf lettuce with a pungent, sometimes bitter flavor.

Om Cafe

23136 N. Woodward (3 1/2 blks. n. of 9 Mile),
Ferndale. 548-1941. L,D. $
Vegetarian, including macrobiotic dishes. Unfussy
setting doesn't diminish one whit the veggie Mexican
specialties, spicy creole tofu jambalaya, or fresh
soups such as great northern bean. For dessert,
strawberry-tofu cheesecake and peach cobbler.

On Stage

48 W. Adams (at Grand Circus Park), Detroit.
965-2920. L,D. $$$
Aptly named, since stage sets are used for dining
areas. Menu is printed like a playbill. Veal Improv
changes daily, but items such as filet mignon, baby
back ribs, and chicken-shrimp brochette are standing
acts. Dessert gets top billing, which is what most
after-theatre crowds want anyway. (The Fox is right
around the corner.)   ☆ ☆

One 23

123 Kercheval (bet. Moross & Cadieux), Grosse
Pointe Farms. 881-5700. L,D. $$$
Heavens, a dazzling contemporary eatery in staid
Grosse Pointe. Westsiders are even driving eastward.
Salmon cakes, goat cheese pizza, grilled mahi mahi,
a potpourri of steamed vegetables, and maybe the
best creme brulee in town—or anywhere for that
matter. Chic but comfy bar and dining room suited
to every attire from tuxedos to blue jeans. (Well,
nice blue jeans.)   ☆ ☆ ☆

Onigaming Supper Club

U.S. 41 (2 mi. s. of Houghton), Chassell.
(906) 482-2714. D. $$
Former yacht club turned restaurant. Planked Lake
Superior trout, steak, barbecued ribs, quail. Fine
dining, but not stuffy. Open May to October.

A Cruvinet is a storage system for preserving opened bot-
tles of wine. This service allows a customer the opportu-
nity to order just one glass of something rare or special.
Some of the most interesting wines "on tap" are at Opus
One in Detroit.

In descending order, the top Russian caviars are beluga,
osetra, and sevruga. As wine and caviar merchant Ed
Jonna says, just remember the acronym BOS.

Opus One

565 E. Larned (bet. Beaubien & St. Antoine),
Detroit. 961-7768. L,D. $$$$
Luxury eatery is named for famous red wine jointly
produced by Robert Mondavi and Chateau Mouton-
Rothschild, and you can bet it's on the Cruvinet.
Miles of imported Italian marble, yards of etched
glass, heavily padded chairs and napkins starched so
stiffly they're hard to unfold. Chef Peter Loren's
approach is French-influenced American cooking
and, for dessert, anything chocolate. Hallmark
appetizer is beignets of bay scallops with Bearnaise.
Lively bar scene. ☆ ☆ ☆ ☆

Original Pancake House, The

20273 Mack (bet. 7 & 8 Mile), Grosse Pointe
Woods. 884-4144. B—all day. $
Some things you just take for granted: fresh-
squeezed orange juice, bracing coffee, the Big Apple
"pancake" and a line out the door. Fans never tire
of oven-baked omelets or French toast with strawberry preserves. Other locations at 1360 S. Woodward, bet. 14 Mile & Lincoln, Birmingham,
642-5775; 19355 W. 10 Mile, Southfield,
357-3399. ☆ ☆

O'Sullivan's Eatery & Pub

1122 S. University (bet. E. University & Church),
Ann Arbor. 665-9009. B,L,D. $
Atmosphere of an Irish pub, though the actual restaurant seats 100. Shepherd's pie, fish & chips, Irish
stew, and Guinness Stout on tap. Sandwiches and
broiled seafood, plus 37 imported beers.

Oxford Inn

1214 S. Main (n. of 10 Mile), Royal Oak. 543-5619.
L,D. $$$
White stucco, wood beams and quaint booths look
mighty English, but menu is American roadhouse.
Specialties are prime rib and baby back ribs. Fresh
catches listed on specials card. A neighborhood
spot. ☆

Reservations, especially at the finer restaurants, are man-
datory on weekends. In booking a table in advance, ask
the name of the reservation taker. Just in case.

Paint Creek Cider Mill and Restaurant

4480 Orion Rd. (bet. Adams & Rochester), Goodison. 651–8361. L,D. Sun. Brunch. $$$

Site itself is museum of Michigan history, not to mention a dining treat. Giant logging wheels, the ship's bell from Tashmoo, and an Indian statue from the old Hedges Wigwam on Woodward are displayed. Rustic dining room is even lit by original Thomas Edison light bulbs. Baked whitefish with capers, sauteed shrimp with sun-dried tomatoes, poached Norwegian salmon in white wine. Breads and desserts are homemade. Popular Sunday brunch.   ☆ ☆

Palace Grille and Lounge, The

at The Palace of Auburn Hills, 3777 Lapeer (exit I-75 at Lapeer Rd./M-24), Auburn Hills. 377-8452. L,D. $$$

Grilled Norwegian salmon, snails in garlic butter and rack of lamb are not exactly standard arena food, but after all, this is the Palace. Elegantly appointed dining room complete with tablecloths, giant booths, and outstanding service. (Call ahead to check hours.)   .☆ ☆ ☆

Panache

555 S. Woodward (bet. Lincoln & 15 Mile), Birmingham. 642-9400. L,D. $$$

Lively bar and dance floor sometimes upstage the dining room. Continental menu touts Veal Oscar, sauteed Dover sole, veal piccata, and seafood fettucine. Lots of wines by the glass.

Panda, The

in Drake Summit Shopping Center, 5586 Drake (at Walnut Lake Rd.), West Bloomfield. 661-1503. L,D. $$

Pretty fancy for chop suey: roomy booths, bone-dry martinis, and a catalog-size Chinese menu. There's no need fiddling with chopsticks; every place setting has forks. Skip the appetizers and head straight for sizzling Polynesian steak or the "Floating Island" of vegetables and snow-white shellfish.   ☆ ☆

Paparazzi
Grand Traverse Resort Village Hotel, U.S. 31 (at M-72), Acme. (616) 938-2100. D. $$
Northern Italian eatery replaces resort's former gourmet Hannah Lay Room. Individual pizzas, veal, homemade pasta, and Caesar salad — a switch to more fun-style eating.

Park Place Cafe
15402 Mack (at Nottingham), Grosse Pointe Park. 881-0550. L,D. $$
A neighborhood tablecloth eatery close to the heart of many a Grosse Pointe maven. GP'ers snap up Tuesday night's lobster special — just $12.95 with drawn butter and new potatoes. Light American menu. Chicken Florentine, sauteed shrimp & scallops in champagne sauce, blackened snapper, and always those delicious little loaves of crunchy millet bread. Serious wine list.   ☆ ☆

Park Terrace Restaurant & Lounge
in Hilton International Windsor, 277 Riverside Dr. W. (opposite Dieppe Park), Windsor, Ontario. (519) 973-4225, (or in Detroit 962-3834). B,L,D. Sun. Brunch. $$$
Groaning buffets at breakfast and lunch; serious a la carte dining at night. Menu focuses on regional Canadian heritage foods such as Essex Cty. fruits, wild game, cheeses, and Ontario wines. Special food festivals provide lots of variety. But let's not forget the view: a spectacular panorama of the Detroit skyline.   ☆ ☆ ☆

Parkside Dining Room
404 Bridge, Charlevoix. (616) 547-9111. B,L,D. $$
Casual all-white lakeside eatery lures families for omelets and blueberry pancakes at breakfast; whitefish, stir-frys, spaghetti, and fresh fruit the rest of the day.   ☆ ☆

Passage to India
3354 W. 12 Mile (bet. Coolidge & Greenfield), Berkley. 541-2119. L,D. $$
Chandeliers, padded chairs, and tuxedoed waiters are dressy touches for tandoori chicken and lamb vindaloo. Excellent mulligatawny soup.   ☆ ☆

Patrick's Shalea Inn
3315 Auburn Rd. (bet. Opdyke & Adams), Auburn Hills. 852-3410. L,D. $$$
Totally rebuilt following a devastating fire, this spot is convenient to the Silverdome and The Palace. Complete dinners include introductory crock of cheese spread, tureen of soup, and salad. Known for pan-fried chicken breast and frog legs. Full line of seafood.   ☆ ☆

Peabody's
154 S. Hunter (at Maple), Birmingham. 644-5222. L,D. $$
Long before family taverns were trendy, there was Peabody's, currently nearing the end of its second decade. Known for long lines, ribs, peel-and-eat shrimp, prime rib, and fresh fish. Late-night menu from 11:30 to 1.   ☆ ☆

Peacock, The
4045 Maple (at Lanson), Dearborn. 582-2344. L,D. $$
You know it's good when you can smell the spices from the parking lot across the street. Excellent tandoori mixed grill, Indian breads, Lamb Palak (with spinach), biryanis (rice dishes), and Palak Paneer (curried chopped spinach with homemade cheese). Lunch buffet.   ☆ ☆ ☆

Peanut Barrel, The
521 E. Grand River (bet. Division & Bailey), E. Lansing. (517) 351-0608. L,D. $
Best burger on campus (well, across from MSU), say local critics. Everything from a hand-patted olive burger to the popular mushroom burger. Jammed on football Saturdays. A dozen imported bottled beers.   ☆ ☆

Pegasus at the Fisher
in the Fisher Building, 3011 W. Grand (at Second), Detroit. 875-7400. L,D. $$
Predictable Greektown food basks in elegant art deco setting of marble and brass. You don't expect tablecloths and comfortable padded chairs either. Excellent lentil soup, salads, and rice pudding. Bar draws smart crowd. Also Pegasus Taverna at 558 Monroe, Detroit, 964-6800.   ☆

Peking House

215 S. Washington (1 blk. s. of 11 Mile), Royal Oak. 545-2700. L,D. $$
Large, brightly lit dining room sports new mauve paint job; menu is pretty au courant, too. Steamed whole fish with ginger and scallions, sizzling sliced tenderloin with black mushrooms, and spicy Mongolian chicken. ☆ ☆

Peppina's Ristorante

1128 Dix (bet. Outer Drive & Southfield), Lincoln Park. 928-5523. L,D. $$
A favorite with downriver families for more than 30 years. On weekends, the crush at the door never lets up. Pizza's the thing, but extensive menu also offers onion focaccia, fried calamari, homemade pastas, charbroiled chicken, veal marsala, and fresh banana cream pie. Owner's collection of stones and minerals lends personal touch. (Closed Monday.) ☆ ☆

Phoenicia

588 S. Woodward (s. of Maple), Birmingham. 644-3122. L,D. $$
The most fashionable ethnic eatery in Metro Detroit with consistently delicious Lebanese specialties and interesting wine list. Some Middle Eastern dishes are adapted to Pritikin guidelines. Unusual specialty is barbecued ribs at Monday dinner and Saturday lunch. Shawarma sandwiches on Monday, Wednesday, and Saturday. ☆ ☆ ☆

Picano's

3775 Rochester Rd. (at Troywood bet. 16 & 17 Mile), Troy. 689-8050. L,D. $$
A 200-seat eatery that thinks it's a small, gourmet hideaway. Pesto sauce, spiedini, homemade rolls, and wispy scallion garnishes are rare touches at family prices. Ditto for grilled lamb chops with rosemary, and Norwegian salmon. Lots of flair. ☆ ☆ ☆

Pickle Barrel Deli

in Evergreen Plaza, 19801 W. 12 Mile (at Evergreen), Southfield. 557-8899. B,L,D. $
Traditional Jewish deli with miniature barrels of "old" and "new" dills at every table. Enormous menu highlighted by delicious sweet noodle kugel and bobka (sour cream coffeecake). ☆ ☆

Pietro's Ristorante and Pizzeria

2780 Birchcrest S.E. (off 28th St., 1 blk. w. of Breton), Grand Rapids. (616) 452-3228. L,D. $$
Main dining room is Northern Italian; casual pizzeria (deep-dish Chicago-style) also specializes in baked pastas. Seating 400 and founded by Pietro Secchia, father of current U.S. Ambassador to Italy Peter Secchia, this is one of the largest restaurants in Southwest Michigan. Signature dishes are Fettucine Michael (spinach and egg fettucine with sauteed chicken and mushrooms) and shrimp and artichoke linguine. Homemade pastas and breads.

Pike Street Restaurant, The

18 W. Pike (2 blks. e. of Woodward, which becomes Wide Track), Pontiac. 334-7878. L,D. $$$$
What a difference a chef makes. Brian Polcyn transformed ho-hum lunch spot into a top-flight eatery. Salmon in puff pastry with scallop and spinach mousse; roast sea scallops in Parmesan crust with tomato coulis; sauteed veal chop with wild mushroom ragout. Serious wine list.　　　☆ ☆ ☆ ☆

Pinkey's Boulevard Club

110 E. Grand (at E. Jefferson), Detroit. 824-2820. L,D. $$
Former blind pig claims to possess state's first liquor license. Now a haven for boaters and loyal fans of the piano bar. Menu is inexpensive, uncomplicated, and not bad: broiled orange roughy, fish & chips, baby frog legs, New York strip.　　　☆ ☆

Pistachio's

2827 E. Grand River (bet. Okemos & Haggedorn), East Lansing. (517) 351-1551. L,D. Sun. Brunch. $$
Popular spot with MSU professors and local business people. Fresh fish and pasta, plus in-house bakery which produces breads and dangerous desserts like the pistachio pudding nut cookie (all one thing) and double fudge Amaretto brownies.　　☆ ☆

Pizza Papalis Taverna

553 Monroe (at Beaubian), Detroit. 961-8020. L,D. $$
What! No shish kebab? The specialty is Chicago-style deep-dish pizza. Also Italian salads, sandwiches, light entrees.　　　☆ ☆

Pizzeria Uno's of West Bloomfield
6745 Orchard Lake (s. of Maple), West Bloomfield.
737-7242. L,D. $$
All the kids will drive you crazy, but so will the
pizza. "Prima Pepperoni" is so thick with sausage &
cheese and the crust so pastry-like, you need a knife
and fork. Good ribs, spicy chicken, powerful garlic
bread, excellent house salad with a red wine vinai-
grette served in a Grolsch beer bottle. Take ear
plugs. Also at 1321 S. University St., Ann Arbor,
769-1744.   ☆ ☆ ☆

Plunkett's Bar & Grill
28 Chatham E. (bet. Goyeau & Ouellette), Windsor,
Ontario. (519) 252-3111. L,D. $
Arrive thirsty. Beer is the specialty — some 20 to 30
different international brands, plus unusual suds on
tap. Casual tavern is adjacent to Chez Vins Bistro
Bistro (same owners). Good soups, creative sand-
wiches, fabulous sausage, hand-patted burgers with
herb seasonings.   ☆ ☆

Polish Village Cafe
2990 Yemans (e. of Jos. Campau & s. of Caniff),
Hamtramck. 874-5726. L,D. $
Elbow-room only at lunch. Everybody comes for
stick-to-the-ribs bean soup, roast pork, boiled
pierogi, and mashed potatoes with genuine lumps.
Sturdy rye bread demands aerobic tug to pull apart.
Ears require muffs.   ☆ ☆

Polonia
2934 Yemans (at Jos. Campau), Hamtramck.
873-8432. B,L,D. Sun. Brunch. $
Old-world atmosphere and real home cooking. Team
of Polish ladies pinches all those pierogi and stuffs
the fresh kielbasa. Make it easy on yourself: order
the combination plate for a taste of everything. ☆ ☆

Sommelier is just a fancy name for wine steward. Three
of the most notable ones in Detroit are Madeline Triffon
of the London Chop House, Claudia Tyagi of The Whit-
ney, and Bob Campbell of the Westin Hotel.

Several downtown restaurants and bars offer complimen-
tary shuttle service to and from the theatres and Joe Lewis
arena. Call ahead.

Pontchartrain Wine Cellars

234 W. Larned (bet. Shelby & Washington), Detroit.
963-1785. L,D. $$$

Detroit had its own French bistro many years before
the craze ever hit. A warm, sophisticated atmos-
phere that contemporary designers would be hard-
pressed to duplicate. Seems Cold Duck, gazpacho,
chicken livers en brochette, perch and pot de creme
have always been on the menu. Ditto for French
wine, foreign waiters, and gracious hospitality of
owners Joe and Mollie Beyer. Popular downtown
lunch spot.   ☆ ☆

Portside Inn

3455 Biddle (bet. Pennsylvania & Eureka), Wyan-
dotte. 281-6700. L,D. $$$

Downriver's "London Chop House." Busy riverside
spot with view of passing freighters and scads of
recreation boats, many of which tie up at the restaurant. American menu of steaks, ribs, and seafood.

                                                        ☆ ☆

Potpourri Cafe

34637 Grand River (bet. Farmington & Drake),
Farmington. 478-8484. L,D. $$

Name certainly fits if you notice the rainbow of
colors, pillows, Fiesta ware, and '50s collectibles.
Deli sandwiches and light entrees at lunch, but more
serious Beef Wellington, shrimp primavera, and
grilled salmon at dinner.   ☆ ☆

Prickly Pear Bar & Grille, The

1113 Ruddiman (off US 31), North Muskegon.
(616) 744-4600. L,D. $$

Southwest theme with view of Lake Muskegon.
Known for Texas white chili, California pork pistachio, mesquite-grilled salmon, and Texas bourbon
steak. Adjacent deli and ice cream parlor cater to
boaters. Breakfast on Saturday and Sunday. Jazz
club Wednesday through Sunday.

Most entrees:		No stars	Not Rated
$	= less than $7	☆	Good
$$	= $7 to $13	☆ ☆	Very Good
$$$	= $13 to $19	☆ ☆ ☆	Excellent
$$$$	= $19 or more	☆ ☆ ☆ ☆	Outstanding
		☆ ☆ ☆ ☆ ☆	Superb
See p. xi for explanations.			

Punchinello's
184 Pierce (s. of Maple), Birmingham. 644-5277.
L,D. $$$
Like dining in a fish bowl—a nice fish bowl—with
all those windows. But not to worry: it's
Birmingham-chic. Mark Davis' menu is a mixed bag
of country French, Italian and whatever else he
personally likes. Hence, polenta flavored with gor-
gonzola or terrific sardines and onions. Delicious
grilled steaks and turkey breast filets.   ☆ ☆ ☆

Pure n' Simple
2791 Rochester (at I-75), Troy. 528-0840. L,D. $
No dairy, no fish, no chicken, no refined sugar.
And no smoking! Creative vegetarian cuisine is sup-
plied by Seventh Day Adventists. Canneloni, vegeta-
ble fritters, pizzas every Thursday night. Sand-
wiches, salads, and all natural desserts such as apple
crisp and pear cobbler. (Closed Saturday.)   ☆ ☆

Quattro Punti
535 Griswold, Buhl Building (at Congress), Detroit.
961-0400. B,L,D. $
A cafeteria minus steamtable mentality. Fresh fish,
pasta, and burgers are prepared to order..Unusual
"line" food includes Louisiana crabcakes, lemon-
pepper scrod, and Cajun-cornmeal catfish. Save
room for lethal chocolate-frosted brownies.   ☆ ☆ ☆

R.I.K.'s the Restaurant
in Orchard Mall, 6303 Orchard Lake (at Maple),
West Bloomfield. 855-9889. L,D. $$$
Initials stand for owners Rick Halberg, Ira Mondry,
and Ken Fink, who also operate R.I.K.'s Total Cuisine Center at Telegraph and Maple. Atmosphere is
casual, cuisine's country Italian. Pizza with escarole,
roasted peppers in olive oil, rabbit braised in red
wine sauce, and tiramisu (espresso-soaked lady fin-
gers layered with mascarpone cheese and shaved
chocolate). Great selection of new-generation Italian
wines.   ☆ ☆ ☆ ☆

R.P. McMurphy's
2922 Biddle (at Oak), Wyandotte. 285-4885. L,D.
$$
Glorified saloon in century-old building furnishes
more than you expect. Daily seafood specials, plus
splash of Mexican for those who can't swear off
nachos. Interesting wines by the glass.   ☆ ☆

Rachelle's on the River

119 Clinton (at Riverside), St. Clair. 329-7159. L,D. Sun. Brunch. $$

Combination classical/new wave atmosphere with emphasis on triangles. They dangle from the ceiling and are repeated with three-cornered buns, burgers, and desserts. Eclectic specialties like Senegalese peanut chicken, whitefish in ginger-almond breading, smoked breast of chicken with homemade fettucine, and the tumble-down "Earthquake Cake" for dessert (guaranteed to smash your diet).

Raja Rani

400 S. Division (at William), Ann Arbor. 995-1545. L,D. $$

Ann Arbor's oldest purveyor of Indian curries, biryanis, chutneys, and chapatis. Buffet at lunch, full menu at night, including tandoori items. Dressy-casual setting in historical old white Victorian house near campus. ☆ ☆ ☆

Rattlesnake Club, The

300 River Place (at the Detroit River), Jos. Campau, Detroit. 567-4400. L,D. $$$

Everything an '80s restaurant should be: electrified atmosphere, contemporary food, snappy service. It took some fine-tuning, but Jimmy Schmidt has his house in order. Main room is dressy; grill is casual; bar is sophisticated. Salmon cakes with cracked mustard sauce, ribeye of beef with onion-mustard compote, spiced baby back ribs with barbecue and swami sauces. Signature desserts are white chocolate ravioli with hazelnut creme anglaise and "Quadruple Chocolate Suicide." (Jackets required in dining room.) ☆ ☆ ☆ ☆

Real Seafood Co., The

341 S. Main (bet. Liberty & William), Ann Arbor. 769-5960. L,D. $$$

Where visiting parents take their college kids to dinner. Large variety of seafood ranging from steamed mussels in garlic butter to lump crab salads and shrimp & swordfish grill.

If you're a vegetarian and dining at an upscale restaurant, it is sometimes best to call ahead and alert the chef. That way you might get something special.

Rhinoceros, The
265 Riopelle (at Franklin), Detroit. 259-2208. L,D.
Sun. Brunch. $$$
Moody, late-night jazz spot with popular piano bar.
Eclectic menu offers a little wild game, a little veal,
a pinch of pasta—whatever happens to be "in" at
the time. But it really doesn't matter what the food
is, the atmosphere's the thing. Even attracts Michigan's Gov. Blanchard. ☆ ☆

Richard & Reiss
273 Pierce (s. of Maple), Birmingham. 645-9122.
B,L,D. $$
Plucky city cafe attracts loyal crowd for hot cereal
and pear-flavored oat bran muffins at breakfast,
assorted sandwiches and salads at lunch, and beef
Wellington at night. Chicken, seafood, and pasta.
Popular meeting place. Lots of carryout. ☆ ☆ ☆

Rikshaw Inn
in Orchard Mall, 6407 Orchard Lake Rd. (at
Maple), West Bloomfield. 851-6400. L,D. $$
David Lum's outlasted everybody on Restaurant
Row—16 years in Metro Detroit's most competitive
dining market. Caesar salad, Mandarin Delight (stir-
fried chicken and beef in oyster sauce), Duck Macao
(crispy fried with bok choy), plus famous shrimp
toast appetizer. ☆ ☆

Ristorante di Maria
2080 Walnut Lake Rd. (just w. of Inkster), West
Bloomfield. 851-2500. D. $$
Neighborhood haunt surpasses expectations of red
checkered tablecloths. Exciting appetizers (eggplant
Sorentino, spiedini alla Maria, zuppa di clams), and
expert veal and shellfish dishes. Signature entree
combines both: three medallions of veal topped with
three shrimp in olive-lemon sauce. Exciting Italian
wine list. ☆ ☆ ☆

Ristorante di Modesta
in Market Street Shops, 29410 Northwestern Hwy.,
(n. of 12 Mile), Southfield. 358-0344. L,D. $$$
Furs, big jewelry, and sleek haircuts are as de
rigueur as feather-light pastas, risotto, and Pinot
Grigio. A very in-spot; who can resist the chic peach
color scheme and warm hospitality of owners
Manuel and Modesta Chavez? Yes, dahling, they
have tiramisu for dessert. ☆ ☆ ☆

Ristorante la Pasta
in Winchester Mall (at Avon & Rochester Rds.),
Rochester Hills. 656–4802. L,D. $$
Sister restaurant to Scallops in Rochester offers
seafood specials but the main menu is contemporary
Italian: calamari sauteed with garlic, chicken pic-
cata, homemade pastas and sauces, individual piz-
zas, veal parmigiana, and charbroiled filet steak.
Italian wines.

Ritz-Carlton, Dearborn, The
Fairlane Town Center, corner of Hubbard Dr. and
Southfield Expressway, Dearborn. 441–2000. $$$$
The Restaurant – B,L,D. Sun. Brunch. Yardstick of
luxury, manners, and good taste. Dressy main dining
room offers upscale American menu, either a la
carte or prix fixe. Quail eggs baked in brioche,
sweetbreads ragout, veal ribeye with morel cream,
breast of free-range chicken with spinach
linguine. ☆ ☆ ☆ ☆
The Grill Room – L,D. English in feel and food:
prime rib, Yorkshire pudding, and Pimm's Cup No.
1. Dancing and live '40s and '50s music on week-
ends. ☆ ☆ ☆ ☆

River Bistro
in the Westin Hotel, Renaissance Center, Promenade
Level, Detroit. 568–8110. L,D. $$$
It had to happen: a serious American bistro in a
major Detroit hotel. The Westin dumped its posh La
Fontaine and red-velvet trappings for a slick,
California-style eatery that tries to be casual but
slips into starched linen. First thing on the table is a
whole head of roasted garlic for spreading on crusty
bread. Menu's mainly seafood (don't miss the oven-
roasted sea bass with olives and herbs), with a dab
of grilled baby chicken and steak. Wine list excels in
American chardonnays. ☆ ☆ ☆

River Crab
1337 N. River Rd. (3 mi. n. of downtown), St.
Clair. 329–2261. L,D. Sun. Brunch. $$$
The one Chuck Muer eatery that's closest –
literally – to the seafood sultan's heart (Muer lives in
St. Clair). Lovely white-linen room overlooking St.
Clair River. Traditionals such as Charley's Chowder,
Charley's Bucket (Dungeness crab, lobster, mussels,
steamers, corn on the cob, redskin potatoes),
Shrimp Danielle, New York strip, and steamed lob-
ster. Known for Sunday brunch.

Riverside Inn
302 River, Leland. (616) 256-9971. B,L,D. $$$
French-trained chef Kevin Burns offers unusual
breakfasts of gingerbread pancakes with lemon
sauce, rock shrimp omelets with brie, and sauteed
tenderloin tips with bordelaise sauce. Lunches are
carryout only, but sit-down dinners range from
Michigan brook trout with tomato-chive beurre
blanc to rack of lamb with Bearnaise.

Roma Cafe
3401 Riopelle (at Erskine), Detroit. 831-5940. L,D.
$$$
A Detroit legend. Red checkered tablecloths, career
waiters in tuxedoes, and staunchly loyal patrons
can't get enough of Hector Sossi's veal Parmesan,
veal piccante, fettucine alfredo, and one of the best
vegetable plates in the city. Love that spinach sauteed with garlic.   ☆ ☆ ☆

Romagnoli's
U.S. 2, Iron Mountain. (906) 774-7300. L,D. $$
Italian family restaurant. Steaks, homemade pasta,
ravioli, gnocchi, veal, and fish.

Rowe Inn, The
Ellsworth-E. Jordan Rd. (Cty. Rd. 48, 1 mi. e. of
Ellsworth), Ellsworth. (616) 588-7351. D. $$$$
Owner Wes Westhoven has been showcasing top-tier
Michigan regional cooking longer than anybody.
Pecan-stuffed morels, grilled duck with wild black-
berry sauce, sorrel soup, and daily vegetarian spe-
cials. Entree price includes four courses. Menu
changes daily. Extensive wine list.   ☆ ☆ ☆ ☆

Rugby Grille
in the Townsend Hotel, 100 Townsend (bet. Pierce
& Henrietta), Birmingham. 642-5999. B,L,D. $$$$
Elegant English grill, well-endowed in marble and
mahogany. Showy sandwich buffet at lunch (tender-
loin carved to order); high-brow grill menu at night.
Filet mignon, salmon, veal chops, and a whale of a
whitefish filet. Intimate bar draws elite crowd.
Afternoon tea 3 to 5 p.m. Tuesday-Saturday. ☆ ☆ ☆

Rupperts'
38 N. Shore Dr. (at the river), South Haven.
(616) 637–5123. L,D. $$$
Resort home converted to a restaurant does a paltry
300 to 500 dinners a night in peak tourist season!
View of Black River inspires mainly seafood menu:
pan-fried lake perch, green lip mussels, seafood
etoufee, lobster with shrimp in white wine-herb
sauce. Steaks and pastas, too.

Sahara
16415 E. Warren (at Outer Drive), Detroit.
885–5503. L,D. $$
Called "the Middle East of the Midwest." Unassum-
ing storefront is perennial Lebanese favorite. Kibbee
nyee, shish kafta, and baba ghanouge.   ☆ ☆

Salvatore Scallopini
*1650 E. 12 Mile (1 blk. w. of Dequindre), Madison
Heights. 542–3281. L,D. $*
Lots of charm; heaps of value. Succinct menu offers
antipasti, soups, pastas, and sauces, all with families
in mind. Combo plates such as lasagna and eggplant
Parmesan; gnocchi and ravioli; veal Parmesan and
fettucine alfredo. Other locations: 505 N. Wood-
ward (at Harmon), Birmingham, 644–8977; 3227
Miller Rd. (I-75 exit), Flint, 732–1070; 29110 Frank-
lin Rd. (lower level of Norm's Oyster Bar & Grill at
Northwestern Hwy.), Southfield, 357–8877; 2650
Orchard Lake (bet. Cass Lk. Rd. & Middlebelt),
Sylvan Lake, 682–5776; 43734 Schoenherr (at
Canal), Sterling Heights, 247–2782.   ☆ ☆

Sandpiper, The
2225 S. Shore Dr. (n. of 32nd St.), Macatawa.
(616) 335–5866. L,D. $$$
Meticulous American cooking with spectacular view
of the marina and harbor. Only yacht missing is
Donald Trump's. Grilled duck with dried cherries
and walnuts; sea scallops with ginger and black-eyed
peas; escargot ravioli; always a gumbo. Main
courses served with 5 to 7 vegetables. Hallmark
dessert is chocolate ravioli filled with dried cherries
and almonds in Amaretto cream.   ☆ ☆ ☆ ☆

Sara's Glatt Kosher Deli

in the New Orleans Mall, 15600 W. 10 Mile (at Greenfield), Southfield. 443-2425. B,L,D. $
Only true kosher deli in Metro Detroit. No-frills atmosphere with all the predictables—brisket of beef, knishes, potato latkes, and chopped liver. Chicken soup "with everything"—kreplach, matzoh ball, and noodles—is wondrous meal in itself. ☆

Scallops of Rochester

1002 N. Main (n. of University), Rochester. 656-2525. D. $$$
Menu suits the nautical theme: everything from shrimp cocktail and Oysters Rockefeller to pan-fried pickerel and grilled swordfish with dill. More formal than family. ☆ ☆

Schnelli Deli

150 Michigan (at Shelby), Detroit. 964-3278. B,L. $
You need sunglasses to block the blinding-orange decor, but count on "schnell" cafeteria service when you're suffering a corned beef attack. There's always a pot of chicken soup on the back burner. Other locations at 16 W. Warren, Detroit, 831-3666; and 59 W. Milwaukee, Detroit, 874-0700. ☆

Schuler's Restaurant

115 S. Eagle (bet. Green & Michigan), Marshall. (616) 781-0600. L,D. Sun. Brunch. $$$
A dining legend, some 80 years strong, where Win Schuler never forgot a customer's name, and where "seconds" of prime rib are always on the house. Roast rib-eye of pork with fresh ginger root glaze, "Little Traverse Chicken," homemade breads and ice cream desserts. Famous brunch buffet. Also at 6020 Ann Arbor Rd., off I-94, Exit 145, Jackson, (517) 764-1200; and 5000 Red Arrow Hwy., off I-94, Exit 23, Stevensville, (616) 429-3273. ☆ ☆ ☆

Sebastian's

in Somerset Mall, 2745 W. Big Beaver, Troy. 649-6625. L,D. $$$
Elegant deco setting with upscale American regional cooking at recently revised bistro prices. Daily-changing menus. Terrine of Ortonville pheasant, salmon cakes with corn sauce, salad of "great grandmother's" wild greens, and chargrilled sea scallops. Great spot to celebrate a sale at Saks. Monthly theme dinners. ☆ ☆ ☆

Seva
314 E. Liberty (bet. 5th & Division), Ann Arbor.
662-1111. L,D. Sun. Brunch. $
Eclectic vegetarian food with a nod to Mexican,
including excellent nachos, chimichangas, black bean
enchiladas, and guacamole. Omelets all day, plus
sinful desserts you know just can't be that healthy.
Variety of beers.   ☆ ☆ ☆

Shannon's Steakhouse
29370 S. River Rd. (1/4 mi. w. of Jefferson), Harri-
son Twp. 469-7111. L,D. $$$
A 32-ounce porterhouse and chateaubriand may be
hallmark dishes but daily seafood specials are
increasingly popular. Charbroiled swordfish steak
with watercress-dill butter, poached salmon in herb
Bearnaise.

Shield's Restaurant . . . Bar . . . Pizzeria
25101 Telegraph (s. of 10 Mile), Southfield.
356-2720. L,D. $$
One of the early purveyors of "Detroit-style" pizza,
meaning square and deep-dish. Sandwiches, pasta,
ribs, and veal. Also at 36863 Van Dyke, at 10 Mile,
Sterling Heights, 979-9270.

Shin Shin Restaurant
978 University W. (bet. Oak & Crawford), Windsor,
Ontario. (519) 252-1449. L,D. $
High altar of Szechuan where the gods are garlic
and hot peppers. Memorable dishes are shrimp with
dried hot pepper sauce, eggplant with hot garlic
sauce, and spicy stir-fried green beans. For a mild
touch, try the steamed Hunan string bun; it pulls
apart like a ball of twine.   ☆ ☆

Siam Spicy
2438 N. Woodward (bet. 12 & 13 Mile), Royal Oak.
545-4305. L,D. $$
Refined Thai cooking as complex as stir-fried
chicken infused with garlic, hot pepper, and basil, or
as simple as fried bean curd with dipping sauce.
Unusual room-temperature salads such as jumbo
shrimp tossed with masses of onion, lemon grass,
green peppers, and lime juice. Informal and
small.   ☆ ☆ ☆

Silky Sullivan's/Kiernan's
21931 Michigan (at Monroe), Dearborn. 565-8975.
L,D. $$$
Popular with Dearborn-area execs on expense
accounts. Same menu in both, though Silky's is the
more formal of the two. Steak, seafood, veal, plus
daily specials that often include wild game.   ☆ ☆

Sindbad's
100 St. Clair (approach from Marquette off E. Jef-
ferson), Detroit. 822-7817. L,D. $
Boaters den can do no sin; clublike clientele will
stand in line forever. View of Detroit River is not
what draws people here (you can hardly see it); it's
the sociable atmosphere, huge filets of pickerel,
groaning plates of New York sirloin, and crispy
fried perch. Breakfast menu available.   ☆ ☆

Sitar
29550 Grand River (1 blk. w. of Middlebelt), Far-
mington Hills. 477-9000. L,D. $$
Complete Indian menu, including Indian beers and
exotic drinks. Haven for vegetarians.

Sleder's
717 N. Randolph, Traverse City. (616) 947-9213.
L,D. $
Oldest continuing operating saloon in the state.
Vintage bar and jukebox, plus original tin ceiling.
Fresh peanuts are from Grandpa Sleder's roaster in
the basement. Menu's the same in the bar or on the
porch: light items like sandwiches, buffalo burgers,
salads, and homemade soups, or main courses such
as seafood, steaks, veal, and chicken.

Snooty Rooster Tea Room, The
601 Pelissier (at Wyandotte), Windsor, Ontario.
(519) 252-0444. B,L, early dinner. $
Not uppity at all. English-country tearoom with
white lace curtains and old oak chairs. Traditional
Brown Betty pots, scones, and a selection of fresh-
baked pies.   ☆

Soho Cafe

439 E. Front (e. of Park), Traverse City.
(616) 947-6463. L. $

Stefani and Jack Parker carry on their wacky, wonderful, non-conformist style of restauraturing in a 400-square-foot storefront whose mustard-yellow paint job gave the city fathers a case of indigestion. It's a mini-clone of the L.A. Cafe in Sylvan Lake which they sold two years ago. Menu ranges from deli sandwiches on "squaw" bread to eclectic salads, daily changing soups, and healthy desserts. Healthy, in fact, is the overall intent. ☆ ☆ ☆

Soup Kitchen, The

1585 Franklin (at Orleans), Detroit. 259-1374. L,D. $

Vintage saloon with good blues, lots of interesting bottled beers, decent sandwiches, and a well-lit parking lot. Soup, of course, is a specialty. Don't be fooled by dinosaur bones. They're actually prime rib bones, but they don't have much "prime" left on them. ☆

Sparky Herberts

15117 Kercheval (bet. Lake Point & Maryland),
Grosse Pointe Park. 822-0266. L,D. Sun. Brunch.
$$$

Prices have been scaled down, but not imagination. Popular eastside haunt has always been strong in appetizers: pesto escargots in tart shells, curried chicken tenderloins, and vegetarian pierogis. Main courses take same eclectic tack. Bar draws mostly singles and serious wine buffs. Ask to see reserve list. ☆ ☆ ☆

Spencer Creek Landing

5166 Helena, Alden. (616) 331-6147. D. $$$

With his next-door casual cafe now closed, owner-chef Jeff Kohl concentrates on high-style dishes served at a relaxed pace. Price of entree includes four courses. Lamb chops with mint pesto, sauteed duck breast in cherry sauce, smoked pork chop with mustard butter. Dessert favorite is citrus sorbet. Menu changes weekly. ☆ ☆ ☆

St. Clair Inn

500 N. Riverside (10 min. e. of I-94), St. Clair. (800) 482-8327 and in Detroit 963-5735. B,L,D. $$$
English tudor hotel overlooks St. Clair River. Dining rooms offer such closeup views of freighter traffic you forget to eat. Safe American menu. Prime rib, pickerel, grilled whitefish, steamed lobster tails, and shrimp & scallop saute. ☆ ☆

Stables, The

416 Fourth (off US-41), Iron Mountain. (906) 774-0890. L,D. $$
An Italian eatery, though you wouldn't know it by the name. The restored 1890s building used to be the stables for a mining company. Gnocchi, polenta, lasagna, steaks, seafood, plus a dab of Oriental stir-fry dishes. Fish-fry every Friday night.

Stafford's Bay View Inn

613 Woodland (1 mi. n. of Petoskey on U.S. 31), Bay View. (616) 347-2771. B,L,D. Sun. Brunch. $$$
Delightful old inn is mostly known for Sunday brunch with hand-carved turkey and ham, waffles, tomato pudding, and bread pudding. Cherished desserts are seven-layer cookies and mini-squares of cheesecake. Daily breakfasts are a treat—red flannel hash, malted waffles, and whole wheat pancakes.
☆ ☆ ☆

Stafford's One Water Street

1 Water St., Boyne City. (616) 582-3434. L,D. $$$
New $2-million dress-up eatery on point jutting into Lake Charlevoix takes the Michigan regional approach: whitefish prepared four different ways, breast of Michigan pheasant, and sirloin of venison.
☆ ☆ ☆

Stafford's Pier

102 Bay, Harbor Springs. (616) 526-6201. L,D. $$$
Clubby dining room and patio overlooking the city dock and Little Traverse Bay. Broiled, chargrilled, or baked-in-parchment whitefish, frog legs, rack of lamb, and free-range chicken. Chic and pretty like the rest of Harbor Springs.

Stage & Co.
on the Boardwalk, 6873 Orchard Lake Rd. (at Maple), West Bloomfield. 855-6622. B,L,D. $$
Such luxury for a deli: full table service, a liquor license (but who drinks at a deli?), servers in semi-formal attire. Corned beef is thickly sliced, pink, and wonderful; potato latkes and roast brisket are possibly the best in town; and ohhh, those wonderful little dinner onion rolls, baked fresh every evening. Sometimes you have to ask for them. ☆ ☆ ☆

Star Deli
24555 W. 12 Mile (w. of Telegraph), Southfield. 352-7377. B,L,D. $
Kosher-style carryout. Top-selling sandwiches are tuna salad and corned beef on twice-baked rye. Also Montreal smoked beef — it's leaner than pastrami, more flavorful than corned beef. ☆ ☆ ☆

Star of Detroit
docked at 20 E. Atwater (at the foot of Hart Plaza), Detroit. 259-9161. L,D. Sat. & Sun. Brunch. $$$$
Modern dining ship cruises to the mouth of Lake St. Clair, then back to the Ambassador Bridge. Buffet features cheeses, fresh fruit, salads, and hot entrees, with a choice of desserts offered at the table.

Star of India
3736 Rochester Rd. (bet. 16 & 17 Mile Rds.), Troy. 528-2517. L,D. $$
Small, unpretentious eatery in strip mall offers Indian menu. Dal and mulligatawny soups, tandoori chicken, lamb vindaloo, and lassi. Lunch buffet.

Steve's Back Room
(in rear of Kalil's Mediterranean), 19872 Kelly (bet. 7 & 8 Mile), Harper Woods. 527-5047. L,D. $$
Finally, Steve Kalil serves his famous Lebanese specials at tableside, not just carryout or wholesale. Marinated fava beans, deliciously creamy feta, vegetarian lentil soup, and piquant kibby neyeh. Pretty but unpretentious. ☆ ☆

Steve's Soul Food
8443 Grand River (bet. W. Grand Blvd. & Joy),
Detroit. 894-3464. B,L,D. $
Contemporary lunchroom atmosphere. The 75-foot
cafeteria line always offers five hot entrees, too
many side dishes to count, plus numerous cakes and
cobblers. Baked macaroni and corn bread are fabulous. Specify carryout or in-house dining.   ☆ ☆

Sugar Bowl
216 W. Main, Gaylord. (517) 732-5524. B,L,D. $$
A Gaylord institution. Though the German decor
suggests bratwurst and sauerkraut, the menu reads
souvlaki, gyros, and roast turkey. A sprawling eatery
known for its braised lamb shanks, broiled white-
fish, and raspberry pie.   ☆

Sultan's
in Robin's Nest Shopping Center, 7295 Orchard
Lake (at Northwestern Hwy.), West Bloomfield.
737-0160. L,D. $$
Smart atmosphere with full array of traditional
Lebanese specialties, plus extras like grilled quail
and, occasionally, wonderful sauteed dandelion
greens with onions. Great vegetarian grapeleaves. If
in doubt what to order, ask owner Walid Eid what
he found special at the market that day.   ☆ ☆ ☆

Summerland
13126 W. Warren (at Schaefer), Dearborn.
584-1105. B,L,D. $$
Plain storefront eatery with short counter and hand-
ful of booths. Who would guess it sells some of the
best shawarma and roasted chickens in Dearborn's
Arabic east end?   ☆ ☆

Summit, The
in the Westin Hotel, Renaissance Center, (bet. Jef-
ferson & Brush), Detroit. 568-8600. L,D. Sun.
Brunch. $$$$
Revolving dining room on Westin's 71st floor has a
view that almost stretches to Sarnia. A steakhouse
with everything from hickory-smoked prime rib to a
42-ounce porterhouse. Entrees come with bucket of
shrimp, chef's potato, unlimited bread, and salad
tossed at tableside. Temporarily closed at time of
publication for remodeling.   ☆ ☆ ☆

Susan Hoffmann Fine Pastries
1219 St. Antoine (at Monroe), Detroit. 965–1692.
L. $
The sweetest three tables in Greektown. Agreed,
that's too small to really qualify as a restaurant, but
in addition to the tempting counter of cheesecakes,
fruit tarts, fruit flans, muffins, and pastries, there
are always lunch-like items. They vary, but might
include quiche, pasta salad, and chicken "torte."
Dee-lish.   ☆ ☆ ☆

Sweet Afton Tea Room
985 N. Mill (nw. of the railroad tracks, n. of Plym-
outh Rd.), Plymouth. 454-0777. L. $
You would have to go to Ontario or the U.K. to
find a better cup of Earl Grey or a Ploughman's
complete with white cheddar from Scotland. Tea is
imported from Fortnum & Mason's in London, but
lemon curd is prepared in Sweet Afton's small
kitchen. Surprise: there's even zesty Branston pickle
relish. Dining room has too many ruffles and wispy
ribbons to count. Reservations required; no smoking.
                                              ☆ ☆ ☆ ☆

Sweet Lorraine's
29101 Greenfield (N. of 12 Mile), Southfield,
559-5985. L,D. $$$
Eclectic cafe awash in soft pastels and sparing art
deco touches. Sauteed chicken dredged in crushed
pecans; cellophane noodles flavored with Thai
spices. Interesting soups, delicious desserts including
chocolate pate. Moderately priced beers and wines.
Also at 1351 W. 14 Mile, Madison Heights,
585-0627.   ☆ ☆

Sweet Water Wharf
5942 Round Lake Rd. (off US-27), Laingsburg.
(517) 651-5096. L,D. $$$
Large eatery (formerly Club Roma) with entertain-
ment on weekends and huge dance floor geared to
guests age 25 and older. Steak, beef Wellington,
Cajun catfish, scallops Alfredo.

Don't for one second think the nightly special will be the
least expensive item on the menu. Often, it's just the
opposite. Ask the price.

Sze-Chuan Restaurant

45188 Ford (at Canton Center Rd.), Canton.
459-3960. L,D. $$
Another glorified storefront, but this one has a
liquor license. Exciting Szechuan and Hunan dishes,
including fiery General Tsou's chicken and spicy
shredded beef in ginger-garlic sauce. Latest twists are
Szechuan and Hunan treatments of lamb.

Szechuan Garden

950 Wyandotte W. (bet. Oak & Crawford), Wind-
sor, Ontario. (519) 253-9595. L,D. $$
Maybe Windsor's best-kept Chinese secret. A
Toronto-sophisticated dining room, impeccable service and irresistible spicy dishes at a surprisingly low
ticket. Cream of corn soup, General Tsou's chicken,
filet of sole with garlic sauce, and bean curd village-
style. Full bar.   ☆ ☆ ☆

Tabor Hill Restaurant

185 Mt. Tabor Rd. (at Exit 16 in Bridgman, off I-
94), Buchanan. (616) 422-1161. L,D. Sun. Brunch.
$$
Vineyards of Tabor Hill Winery are visible from
contemporary dining room attached to retail shop.
Mesquite-grilled shrimp, sauteed shrimp & scallops
on spinach pasta, prime rib. Best sips are Tabor
Hill's Riesling and Chardonnay. Closed Monday and
Tuesday.

Tapawingo

9502 Lake St. (Cty. Rd. 48, 1 mi. e. of Ellsworth),
Ellsworth. (616) 588-7971. D. $$$$
Distinguished regional cooking by Harlan (Pete)
Peterson, who is carving a niche in the national
food scene as well as Michigan's. Smoked whitefish
mousse, herbed lamb loin with red pepper pasta,
duck burrito with lingonberry sauce. Entree price
includes three courses. Frequently changing menu.
Extensive wine list.   ☆ ☆ ☆ ☆

Ted's

885 Opdyke (n. of Silverdome), Auburn Hills.
373-4440. L,D. $$
Convenient den for Lions fans. Sprawling bar/
restaurant is known for seafood "steaks" (halibut,
swordfish, salmon), but also beefy porterhouses.
Pizza, soups, burgers.   ☆ ☆

Terrace Inn

216 Fairview (bet. Lakeview & Encampment), Bay View. (616) 347-2410. L,D. $$$

Worth the trip for chef Scott Schaeffer's elaborate presentation of Northern Michigan's hallmark dish, planked whitefish: a large filet, ringed with duchess potatoes, baked and served on a hardwood slab. In nice weather, the Terrace Inn, dubbed "the Little Grand" because of its resemblance to the Grand Hotel on Mackinac Island, serves dinner on the porch. Pork tenderloin in pecan-mustard sauce, jumbo butterflied shrimp with crabmeat stuffing, lamb chops brushed with honey-mustard glaze.   ☆ ☆ ☆

Terry's Place

101 Antrim, Charlevoix. (616) 547-2799. D. $$

Continental-style spinoff of owner-chef Terry Left's casual Great Lakes Fish & Chips. Single-biggest seller is Whitefish Duglier (poached in cream sauce); other choices are pasta, steak, escargot, and duck.

Terry's Terrace

36470 Jefferson (at Crocker), Mt. Clemens. 463-2671. B,L,D. $

The prices are so moderate that people like to keep the place a secret. A large, sprawling family tavern where whitefish, blue marlin, halibut, tuna, and boat loads of other fresh catches cost less than $10. Premium wines even wear an inexpensive tag. Always jammed. Ear protection recommended. ☆ ☆

Thai Classic Cuisine

1945 King (at Fort St.), Trenton. 675-4288. L,D. $$

Bright, squeaky-clean dining room of Chalong and Maria Harnphanich. Complete Thai menu, including soups ladled from steaming firepots, beef satay, assorted fish tickled with Thai spices or sauced with curries, and homemade coconut ice cream.   ☆ ☆

Most entrees:		No stars	Not Rated
$	= less than $7	☆	Good
$$	= $7 to $13	☆ ☆	Very Good
$$$	= $13 to $19	☆ ☆ ☆	Excellent
$$$$	= $19 or more	☆ ☆ ☆ ☆	Outstanding
		☆ ☆ ☆ ☆ ☆	Superb
See p. xi for explanations.			

Thai House
25223 Gratiot (at 10 Mile), Roseville. 776–3660.
L,D. $$
An ethnic eatery with as many flavors of the culture
as the cuisine. Warm hospitality of owner Pipop
Leodhuvaphan and displays of his family's personal
photographs, coins, sculptures, and jewelry add to
the interesting flavors of the food. Long menu of
Thai salads (served at room temperature), appe-
tizers, curries, and stir-frys. The only concession to
foreign palates is the spice level: for those of timid
taste, there's "extra mild."   ☆ ☆ ☆

Thai Inn
*in South Hill Plaza, 900 S. Rochester Rd., Roches-
ter. 656–0287. L,D. $$*
Not to worry, menu is fully translated, and Thais
never use chopsticks (though they are available).
White table linens accent artful presentations of
chicken, beef, seafood, and vegetarian entrees.
Appetizers include satay, spring rolls, and a marvelous potato-chicken pastry called Kalipop. Delicious
soups, homemade coconut ice cream, and Thai iced
coffee. Courteous service. Full bar.   ☆ ☆ ☆

Thomas Edison Inn
*500 Thomas Edison Parkway (beneath the Bluewater
Bridge), Port Huron. 984–8000. B,L,D. $$$*
Luxurious new motor lodge with huge dining room
facing Blue Water Bridge. Menu focuses on fresh
American ingredients. Broiled whitefish, grilled
pickerel, rainbow trout creole, charbroiled lamb
chops.

Thornapple Village Inn
*445 Thornapple Village Dr. (SE corner of Ada Dr.
at Fulton), Ada. (616) 676–1233. L,D. $$$*
Bi-level dining rooms overlook spacious grounds and
Thorn Apple River. Very proper country motif is
accented with American antiques. Baked Norwegian
salmon on braised romaine with red pepper butter;
fresh rainbow trout with lemon-chive cream; rack of
lamb with Bearnaise. Entree includes fresh baby
vegetables and homemade whole wheat bread.
Casual menu in Tap Room specializes in deep-dish
pizza.

333 East
Omni Hotel, 333 E. Jefferson (e. of Woodward),
Detroit. 222-7404. B,L,D. $$$
Homogenized hotel approach seems to have won out
over the new American cuisine and serious wine
program that heaped glory on the Omni when it
opened. Buffet and a la carte menu at lunch; pan-
fried lake perch, Maryland crab cakes, veal scalop-
pini, and Cajun-style pork chops at dinner.

Tidewater Grill
Eastland Center (on Vernier, w. of I-94), Harper
Woods. 527-1050. L,D. $$
Familiar with D. Dennison's on the far west side?
Tidewater has the same owner and menu's a clone.
Seafood, with extra dollops of chicken and pasta.
Casual; good family spot. ☆ ☆

Tokyo Sushi-Iwa
22601 Allen Rd. (at West Rd.), Woodhaven.
676-4721. L,D. $$$
No big surprise: The sprawling $2.5-million Japanese
eatery was put there to entertain executives of the
nearby Mazda plant. A 17-seat sushi bar, regular
seating for 250, and tatami rooms reflect the com-
mitment. Fixed price and a la carte dining. Sushi,
sashimi, sukiyaki, shabu shabu, tempura. A small
branch of this eatery is located in the Hyatt Regency
next to Giulio & Sons, Dearborn, 336-6666. ☆ ☆ ☆

Tom's Oyster Bar
15016 Mack (near Alter Rd.), Grosse Pointe Park.
822-8664. D. $$
Bare wood floors and dozens of old framed New
Yorker magazine covers keep pretense to a minimum. But there's no shortage of pride when it
comes to the assortment of fresh oysters, variety of
charbroiled seafood, or array of bottled beers. Mobs
of adoring eastsiders wait forever for a table. ☆ ☆ ☆

Tosi's
4337 Ridge (near Gaylord Rd.), Stevensville.
(616) 429-3689. L,D. $$$
For 50 years, the personal "country club" of St. Joe-
Benton Harbor area. Amazing creativity for such a
large Italian eatery: Ligurian pizza, veal-stuffed
agnolotti (similar to ravioli), peppered filet mignon,
grilled Provimi veal chop. Huge wine list, mostly the
fine Italian sort.

Traffic Jam & Snug
Canfield at Second (2 blks. w. of Woodward),
Detroit. 831-9470. L,D. $$
Nobody pulls as many surprises as TJ's. It's a
licensed dairy (makes its own cheese and ice cream),
a bakery (produces unusual breads and cookies
every day), a charcuterie (processes and smokes own
sausages), and is about to open a brewery in the
parking lot across the street. Food is light, seasonal,
often vegetarian. Desserts, though, are decadent. Au
courant wines at bargain prices. Monday—lunch
only. ☆ ☆ ☆ ☆

Traiteurs Bistro
656 Pitt W. (bet. Caron & Janet), Windsor, Ontario.
(519) 258-2293. L,D. $$$
Maybe a mishmash when it comes to decor, but
chef-operated eatery has its menu in order. A
French-Mediterranean slant to salads, soups, rack of
lamb, loin of veal, chicken, and seafood. Fabulous
pies made from local fruit. Nice selection of Canadian wines and beers. ☆ ☆

Treasure Island
924 N. Niagara (off Holland), Saginaw.
(517) 755-6577. L,D. $$$
Riverfront setting, including patio. Caters to busi-
ness types at lunch. Dinners feature fresh fish, prime
rib, lobster, and deep-fried ice cream ball.

Trevi
518 Goyeau (across from Windsor-Detroit tunnel),
Windsor, Ontario. (519) 253-7448. L,D. $
Canned green beans may not cut the mustard, but
the pizza sure does—a medium-thick crust with a
blush of tomato sauce, weighted down with a ton of
slivered pepperoni. Extremely clean and stylish white
stucco and wood dining room. ☆

Trillium
Grand Traverse Resort Village Hotel, U.S. 31 (at M-
72), Acme. (616) 938-2100. L,D. Sun. Brunch. $$$
Resort's dress-up dining room with 16th floor view
of Grand Traverse Bay. Brass rotisserie spins out
roast duck, peppered sirloin, shrimp, and lobster. ☆ ☆

Tug's
2299 Elizabeth Lake (3 blks. w. of Telegraph), Pontiac. 683-7585. L,D. $$
Family tavern with emphasis on sandwiches and seafood. Owner Ben Pearlman (former proprietor of Benjie's in Sylvan Lake) makes sure there's a sizable list of fresh catches, but also a decent burger smothered with grilled onions and a tasty slab of Cajun ribs. ☆ ☆

Tunnel Bar-B-Q
58 Park St. E. (at Freedom Way), Windsor, Ontario. (519) 258-3663. B,L,D. $
TBQ may be famous for cheesecakes, pies, and tortes, and of course, the barbecued ribs, but breakfast is still a highlight. One of the few Canadian eateries that offers peameal bacon. And oh, those marvelous home-fried potatoes! They're even better. Expect a line on Saturday morning. ☆ ☆

220 Merrill Street
220 Merrill (at Woodward), Birmingham. 645-2150. L,D. $$
Right in the heart of downtown Birmingham, the lively bar overshadows dining room. Menu is a mixed bag: everything from German potato pancakes and bratwurst to a Maurice salad bowl and grilled steak sandwich. ☆

Uncle Harry's Deli and Restaurant
21809 Greater Mack (bet. 8 & 9 Mile), St. Clair Shores. 775-3120. L,D. $
One of the few Jewish delis on the east side. Immaculate and neighborly, with scads of family photos on the wall. Corned beef and tuna sandwiches, homemade soups including award-winning minestrone, and cream pies. ☆ ☆

Under the Eagle
9000 Jos. Campau (3 blks. s. of Holbrook), Hamtramck. 875-5905. L,D. $
A tad more formal than the rest of Hamtramck's ethnic eateries. Soups are high points: duck's blood, creamy dill pickle, and cabbage. Also delicious pan-fried cheese and potato pierogi. Closed Wednesday.

☆ ☆

Union Street

4145 Woodward (bet. Alexandrine & Willis),
Detroit. 831-3965. L,D. $
Bustling saloon convenient to Wayne State and the
medical center with a munchie menu of salads, sandwiches, seafood, steaks, and burgers. Eclectic variety
ranges from buffalo burgers to jambalaya. Daily
dessert specials and many imported beers. ☆

Ups n' Downs English Parlours

226 N. Front (bet. Lochiel & George), Sarnia,
Ontario. (519) 336-0337. L,D. $$
English pub/restaurant complete with steak & kid-
ney pie, shepherd's pie, bubble & squeak, steak,
lamb chops, and Guinness Stout on tap. View over-
looks St. Clair River.

Valente's Little Italy

227 Hutton (at Dunlap), Northville. 348-0575. D.
$$$
Scrapbook family pictures and faded war memorabi-
lia create a personal atmosphere in the homey old
farmhouse that used to be Elizabeth's. Appetizers of
lemony spiedini and paper-thin melanzane ripieni
(rolled eggplant), plus Northern Italian-inspired veal,
chicken, and seafood main courses. Intimate table is
the one under the stairwell. Serious Italian wine
list. ☆ ☆ ☆

Van Dyke Place

649 Van Dyke (off E. Jefferson), Detroit. 821-2620.
D. $$$$
Impeccable turn-of-the-century elegance of restored
William Muir Finck home matches lavish menu of
veal chops stuffed with sweetbread mousse, beef
tenderloin in port wine sauce, and poached Maine
lobster with pink grapefruit. A special occasion
place where reservations are mandatory. ☆ ☆ ☆ ☆

Vannelli Gus' Steak House

801 S. Lapeer (n. of Clarkston Rd.), Lake Orion.
693-8882. L,D. $$$
Comfortable farmhouse atmosphere with white
linens at lunch and dinner. Dante Vannelli calls his
menu three-tiered: (1) fresh fish, (2) steaks & chops,
and (3) pastas, veals, and chicken. Signature items
are the "red" sweet & sour salad dressing, bacon-
fried potatoes, and prime rib.

Victorian Inn, The
1229 Seventh St. (at Union), Port Huron. 984–1437.
L,D. $$$
Lovely restored house, typical of the town's dwin-
dling number of turn-of-the-century Queen Anne
homesteads. Dining room is dressed in white linen
and vintage china. To-the-point American menu.
Seafood, chicken, veal, and beef. Excellent soups
and house salad. Surprising wine list.   ☆ ☆

Victors'
Campus Inn, 615 E. Huron (at State), Ann Arbor.
769–2282. B,L,D. Sun. Buffet. $$$
Hotel's upscale eatery. Menu is textbook "new
American cuisine": duck and shiitake mushroom
pizza, warm Michigan venison pate, breast of
chicken en croute, and housemade ice creams.

☆ ☆ ☆

Vierling Saloon & Sample Room, The
119 S. Front (at Main), Marquette. (906) 228–3533.
B,L,D. $$
Painfully restored 19th century saloon overlooking
lower harbor. Hearty breakfasts with homemade
bread, waffles, pancakes. Whitefish prepared five
different ways, barbecued ribs, veal Marsala. Guin-
ness Stout on tap.

Village Cafe
3337 Greenfield (at Rotunda), Dearborn. 271–8040.
L,D. $$
American portion of menu keeps growing, but Mid-
dle Eastern is the terra firma. All the predictable
Lebanese appetizers plus delicious main course of
Lamb or Chicken Ghallabba (with rice, onions,
green pepper, and garlic).   ☆ ☆

Vince's
1341 Springwells (n. of I-75), Detroit. 842–4857.
L,D. $$
Unpretentious Italian family eatery that's ventured
far beyond its original pizza days. But, oh, such
pizza! Also veal, homemade pastas, gnocchi, and
intensely flavored tomato sauces.   ☆ ☆

Vivio's
2460 Market St. (Eastern Market), Detroit.
393–1711. B,L,D. $$
Popular market breakfast & bar spot. On weekends,
John Vivio can't dish up enough eggs, thick bacon,
hash browns, breakfast steaks, toast, and Bloody
Marys. By noon, preferences switch to taco salads,
burgers, and steak sandwiches.   ☆

Wagon Wheel Saloon
2950 Rochester Rd. (at Big Beaver), Troy. 689–8194.
L,D. $$
Jam-packed noshing spot boasts rare collection of
original Tiffany glass. Known for "everything-but-
the-kitchen-sink" pizza, nachos, burgers, and tortilla
chips with El Paso dip. Eclectic menu has something
for everybody.   ☆ ☆

Wah Court
2037 Wyandotte W. (off Rankin), Windsor, Ontario.
(519) 254–1388. L,D. $$
Always packed with Chinese customers, which
means it's gotta be good. Known for dim sum,
served daily until 3 p.m. Roaming servers carry trays
of bamboo steamers offering tastes of pork-stuffed
buns, shredded yam balls, itty-bitty barbecued ribs,
and dozens more mysterious but marvelous edibles.
Beyond that, the thick, eggy corn soup is a must,
along with Chinese-style beef tenderloin.   ☆ ☆ ☆

Walloon Lake Inn
8 mi. s. of Petoskey off M-75, Walloon Lake Vil-
lage. (616) 535–2999. D. $$$
Yearly improvements never cease: first new kitchen
equipment, next air-conditioning, then Villeroy &
Boch china. Owner-chef David Beier runs a quiet,
efficient dining room in a charming bed and breakfast overlooking the lake. Daily veal specials and
baked whitefish. He still imports French-style crusty
rolls from Chicago and makes his own ice creams.
                                          ☆ ☆ ☆

Washington Street Station
114 E. Washington (at Main), Ann Arbor.
663–0070. L,D. Sun. Brunch. $$
High ceilings and vintage decor are a contrast to the
contemporary California menu: house-smoked
chicken with wild mushrooms; blue corn chips with
black bean salsa; pan-roasted lamb loin with rata-
touille, pesto, and saratoga chips.   ☆ ☆ ☆

Waterworks Restaurant & Pub

21031 Michigan Ave. (w. of Southfield), Dearborn.
562-6080. L,D. $$
Trendy eatery in original Dearborn waterworks
which also was the workshop of George Washington
Carver. Broad menu including Buffalo wings, char-
grilled steak, and blackened chicken, shrimp, and
beef. Good desserts, courageous wine list.   ☆

West East Ethnic Restaurant

975 Orchard Lake (at Old Telegraph), Pontiac.
334-5980. L,D. $$
A rare restaurant where general manager Nguyen
Huy Han, known simply as "Mr. Han," chooses to
lead a humble existence to pay annual rebates to
customers. Simple but delicious Asian specialties are
dished up as readily as his philosophy of world
harmony. A restaurant worth supporting. Also at
129 N. Perry, Pontiac, 334-5040.   ☆ ☆

Whistle Stop Coffee Shop

501 S. Eton, Birmingham. 647-5588. B,L,D. $
Former Birmingham cop Harold Christie spent so
much time baking here in his off hours, he eventu-
ally retired from the force and bought the place.
Busy breakfast spot with famous toasted homemade
white and whole wheat breads. Simple lunches and
dinners with mountainous homemade pies for
dessert—apple crumb, brandied mincemeat, cherry,
and blueberry.   ☆ ☆

Whitney, The

4421 Woodward (at Canfield), Detroit. 832-5700.
L,D. Sun. Brunch. $$$$
Luxurious old-world elegance, guaranteed to impress
the relatives. Former David Whitney mansion is
home to complex American cooking: veal loin with
chive corn bread dressing, chicken pot pie with fen-
nel, all-natural Colorado beef. Dessert, served in
upstairs drawing rooms, is an extravaganza. Extensive wine list. Popular bar on third floor. A dress-up
place for sure.   ☆ ☆ ☆ ☆

When figuring the gratuity, some people base the amount
on food costs only. It is more customary, however, to tip
on the bottom line.

Windows

*7677 W. Bay Shore Dr. (7 mi. n. of Traverse City
on M-22), Traverse City. (616) 941-0100. L,D. $$$*
American regional cooking with emphasis on Cajun
spices and limitless chocolate desserts. Turtle soup,
Tournedos Marchand du Vin, Veal Wynn Dixie,
barbecued shrimp over linguine, and pecan cheese-
cake. There are plenty of windows overlooking the
bay.   ☆ ☆ ☆ ☆

Wing Hong/Tokyo Japanese
Steakhouse/Tokyo Sushi Bar

*31455 W. 14 Mile (at Orchard Lake), Farmington
Hills. 851-8600. L,D. $$*
Name says it all: whether you feel like fried rice,
sizzling steak, or rolled sushi, there are separate
dining rooms for each. Wood-trimmed sushi bar,
however, is the most inviting. Terrific "California
roll."   ☆ ☆

Wong's Eatery

*1457 University W. (Curry & McKay), Windsor,
Ontario. (519) 252-8814 (or in Detroit 961-0212).
L,D. $$*
Owner Raymond Wong is the rare Chinese restaura-
teur who pays as much attention to trends as tradi-
tion. His dim sum items are usually seafood and
shellfish instead of red meat because "that's how
people are eating today." Known for intricate dishes,
first-class ingredients, and formal service.   ☆ ☆ ☆

Woodbridge Tavern

*289 St. Aubin (at Woodbridge), Detroit. 259-0578.
L,D. Sun. Brunch. $*
Vintage saloon with well-worn hardwood floor and
tin ceiling that, thankfully, haven't been restored.
Burgers, sandwiches, steaks, and fabulous Cobb
salad ribboned with everything from fresh avocado
to blue cheese. Outdoor dining. Entertainment. ☆ ☆

Wooden Spoon Restaurant, The

*309 Chatham W. (at Dougall, 1 blk. s. of Windsor
Hilton), Windsor, Ontario. (519) 252-9472. B,L,D. $*
Unpretentious, home-style cooking complemented by
wonderful multi-grain breads, bran muffins, and
Dutch apple pie from adjoining bakery. Canadian
meat pies, quiche, and hot roast beef sandwiches
have loyal following.   ☆

Wooly Bully's
11310 Hayes (at Kelly), Detroit. 839–8777. L,D. $
Specialties are hot cars from the '50s (a '57 Plymouth protrudes from the front of the building), the jitterbug, and buckets of cold beer and margaritas. Pizza, chili, shoestring potatoes, and Mexican munchies. Where company softball teams chill out. Dinner only at Detroit. Also at 36434 Groesbeck, s. of Metro Pkwy., Mt. Clemens, 792–3444. ☆

Xochimilco
3409 Bagley (at 23rd), Detroit. 843–0179. L,D. $
Sprawling Mexican eatery draws lively young crowd that never settles for one basket of chips or one margarita. Great botanas, chimichangas, and quesadillas. ☆ ☆

Zehnder's
730 S. Main (downtown), Frankenmuth.
(517) 652–9925. B,L,D. $$
All-you-can-eat chicken dinner with everything under the sun: soup, bread, coleslaw, cottage cheese, relish, mashed potatoes, gravy, dressing, noodles, vegetable, and dessert. (Breakfast and Sunday brunch in coffee shop only.)

Zingerman's
422 Detroit (at Kingsley), Ann Arbor. 663–3354.
B,L,D. $
Delis don't come any better. Shrine of corned beef, bagels, kugels, and knishes, plus prosciutto, black forest ham, and countless other sandwich delicacies. Give sandwich No. 45 a try: Farmer Randy's is poached free-range chicken breast with imported swiss cheese and Honeycup mustard on rye. Shop for extra-virgin olive oils, balsamic vinegars, unique cheeses, rice from around the world, and fresh or smoked salmon. Marvelous Jewish rye bread, too. It's impossible to leave empty-handed or hungry. ☆ ☆ ☆ ☆ ☆

Zukin's Deli
2753 Yemans (at Jos. Campau), Hamtramck.
873–2700. B,L. $
Bernie Roberts doesn't care if everybody else in Hamtramck does kielbasa and mashed potatoes. His specialty is a four-decker corned beef and pastrami sandwich—No. 25—that stands a good six inches high. Crusty Jewish rye bread, brisket dinners, matzoh ball soup, and home-cured dills. ☆ ☆

INDEXES

KEY TO GEOGRAPHIC REGIONS

1 Wayne County (includes Detroit)
2 Oakland County
3 Macomb County
4 Ann Arbor & Vicinity
5 Southeastern Lower Peninsula
6 Central Lower Peninsula
7 Western Lower Peninsula
8 Northern Lower Peninsula
9 Upper Peninsula
10 Windsor
11 Sarnia

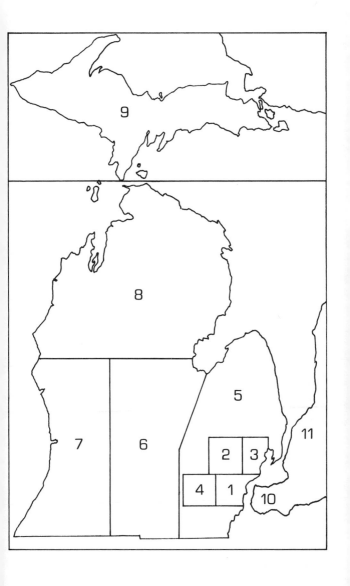

GEOGRAPHIC LISTS

Wayne County
(includes Detroit)

Allen Park
Canton
Dearborn
Detroit
Flat Rock
Garden City
Grosse Pointe
Hamtramck
Harper Woods
Highland Park
Lincoln Park
Livonia
Melvindale
Plymouth
Redford Twp.
Taylor
Trenton
Woodhaven
Wyandotte

Oakland County

Auburn Hills
Berkley
Bloomfield Hills
Clarkston
Clawson
Drayton Plains
Farmington
Farmington Hills
Ferndale
Goodison
Holly
Lake Orion
Madison Heights
Milford
Northville
Novi
Oak Park
Oxford
Pontiac
Rochester
Rochester Hills
Royal Oak
Southfield
Sylvan Lake
Troy
West Bloomfield

Macomb County

East Detroit
Fraser
Harrison Twp.

Hazel Park
Mt. Clemens
Roseville
St. Clair Shores
Sterling Heights
Utica
Warren

Ann Arbor & Vicinity

Canton
Dexter
Dixboro
Plymouth
Ypsilanti

Southeast Lower
Peninsula

Algonac
Blissfield
Flint
Frankenmuth
Lapeer
Monroe
Port Huron
St. Clair

Central Lower
Peninsula

Chesaning
Clare
East Lansing
Jackson
Laingsburg
Lansing
Marshall
Midland
Mt. Pleasant
Okemos
Saginaw
Sterling

Western Lower
Peninsula

Ada
Buchanan
Grand Rapids
Kalamazoo
Macatawa

North Muskegon
Paw Paw
Plainwell
Saugatuck
South Haven
St. Joseph
Stevensville
Union Pier

Northern Lower Peninsula

Acme
Alden
Bay View
Boyne City
Burdickville
Cadillac
Charlevoix
Clare
Cross Village
Ellsworth
Gaylord
Glen Arbor
Harbor Springs
Leland
Mackinac Island
Maple City

Northport
Pellston
Petoskey
Sterling
Suttons Bay
Traverse City
Walloon Lake Village

Upper Peninsula

Blaney Park
Chassell
Copper Harbor
Escanaba
Iron Mountain
Kearsarge
Mackinac Island
Marquette
Munising
Sault Ste. Marie
Seney
St. Ignace

Ontario

Sarnia
Windsor

GEOGRAPHIC INDEXES

Schnelli Deli
Silky Sullivan's
Sindbad's
Soup Kitchen
Sparky Herberts
Star of Detroit
Steve's Back Room
Steve's Soul Food
Summerland
Summit, The
Susan Hoffmann
Sweet Afton Tea Room
Sze-Chuan Restaurant
Thai Classic Cuisine
333 East
Tidewater Grill
Tokyo Sushi-Iwa
Tom's Oyster Bar
Traffic Jam
Under the Eagle
Union Street
Van Dyke Place
Village Cafe
Vince's
Vivio's
Waterworks
Whitney, The
Woodbridge Tavern
Wooly Bully's
Xochimilco
Zukin's

Oakland County

Ah Wok
Alban's
Alibi Lounge
America's Pizza Cafe
Appe'teaser II
Archers
Bangkok Club
Bangkok Express
Beau Jack's
Benno's
Betty Ross II
Beverly Hills Grill
Bijou
Botsford Inn
Bouquets
Bread Basket Deli
Buddy's Pizza
Cafe Cortina
Cafe Jardin
Charley's Crab
Charley's Seafood
  Taverns
Chez Raphael
Clamdigger's
Clarkston Cafe
Confetti's
Cooper's Arms
Country Epicure

Country Jim's
Cucina Di Pasta
D. Dennison's
Deli Unique
Double Eagle
Dunleavy'z
E.G. Nick's
Excalibur
Fox & Hounds
Genitti's
Ginopolis'
Golden Mushroom
Hershel's Deli
Historic Holly Hotel
Hogan's
Home Sweet Home
Houlihan's
Inn Season
Jacques Demers
Kingsley Inn
Kruse and Muer
La Familia
Lark, The
Le Metro
Le Peep
Lepanto
Les Auteurs
Long Branch
Machus Red Fox
Machus Sly Fox
Mackinnon's
Marco's
Mary Ann's Kitchen
Medallion
Metro Musicafe
Michael's
Midtown Cafe
Mitch's Tavern
Mon Jin Lau
Monchelle Lamoure
Murdock's
Musashi
Natraj
Nicky's
Nipponkai
Norm's Oyster Bar
Norman's Eton St.
Oliverio's
Om Cafe
Original Pancake House
Oxford Inn
Paint Creek
Palace Grille, The
Panache
Panda, The
Passage to India
Patrick's Shalea Inn
Peabody's
Peking House
Phoenicia
Picano's
Pickle Barrel
Pike Street

Pizzeria Uno's
Potpourri Cafe
Punchinello's
Pure n' Simple
R.I.K.'s
Richard & Reiss
Rikshaw Inn
Ristorante di Maria
Ristorante di Modesta
Ristorante la Pasta
Rugby Grille
Salvatore Scallopini
Sara's
Scallops
Sebastian's
Shield's
Siam Spicy
Sitar
Stage & Co.
Star Deli
Star of India
Sultan's
Sweet Lorraine's
Ted's
Thai Inn
Tug's
220 Merrill Street
Valente's
Vannelli Gus'
Wagon Wheel Saloon
West East Ethnic
Whistle Stop
Wing Hong

Macomb County

Andiamo
Bangkok Cuisine
Brewery, The
Buddy's Pizza
Cafe Piccirilli
Cloverleaf
Don Carlos
Eddie's Drive-In
Elizabeth's by the Lake
Fairfield's
Farm House, The
Ivy's in the Park
Joe Bologna
Macardy's
Mackinnon's Macomb
  Inn
Meritage, The
Mexican Village
Mr. Paul's
Olde Town Cafe
Salvatore Scallopini
Shannon's
Shield's
Sweet Lorraine's
Terry's Terrace
Thai House

Uncle Harry's
Wooly Bully's

Ann Arbor & Vicinity

Amadeus Cafe
Angelo's
Bella Ciao
Cousins Heritage Inn
Del Rio
Earle, The
Escoffier
French Market Cafe
Gandy Dancer
Gratzi
Haab's
Kerrytown Bistro
Le Peep
Lord Fox
Maude's
Mexican Fiesta
Miki
Moveable Feast, The
O'Sullivan's
Old German
Pizzeria Uno's
Raja Rani
Real Seafood Co., The
Seva
Sze-Chuan Restaurant
Victors'
Washington Street
Zingerman's

Southeast Lower Peninsula

Bavarian Inn
Franconian, The
Frankenmuth Corner
  Tavern
Great Lakes Inn
Hathaway House
Rachelle's
River Crab
Salvatore Scallopini
St. Clair Inn
Thomas Edison Inn
Victorian Inn, The
Zehnder's

Central Lower Peninsula

Beggar's Banquet
Chesaning Heritage
  House
Dusty's
Embers, The

Evergreen Grill
Hotel Doherty
Iva's
Jim's Tiffany Place
Justine
Montague Inn
Peanut Barrel, The
Pistachio's
Schuler's
Sweet Water Wharf
Treasure Island

Western Lower Peninsula

Arie's Cafe
Billie's Boathouse
Bravo!
Carlucci
Clementine's
Clementine's Too
Cygnus
Grande Mere Inn
Little River Cafe
Loaf & Mug
Magnolia Grille
Miller's
1913 Room, The
Oakley's
Pietro's
Prickly Pear, The
Rupperts'
Sandpiper, The
Schuler's
Tabor Hill
Thorn Apple Village
Tosi's

Northern Lower Peninsula

Andante
Arboretum
Bluebird
Boone's
Bower's Harbor Inn
Busia's
Cousin Jenny's
D.J. Kelly's
Dam Site Inn
Diana's Delight
Dill's Olde Town
Fischer's
Glen Lake Inn
Grain Train
Grand Hotel
Great Lakes Whitefish
Hattie's
Hermann's

Homestead, The
Hotel Doherty
Iva's
Juilleret's — Harbor
   Springs
Juilleret's — Charlevoix
Kelly's Road House
La Becasse
Leelanau Country Inn
Legs Inn
Lorien
Paparazzi
Parkside Dining Room
Riverside Inn
Rowe Inn
Sleder's
Soho Cafe
Spencer Creek
Stafford's Bay View
Stafford's One Water St.
Stafford's Pier
Sugar Bowl
Tapawingo
Terrace Inn
Terry's Place
Trillium
Walloon Lake Inn
Windows

Upper Peninsula

Antler's, The
Blaney Inn
Cafe du Voyageur
Crispigna's
Dogpatch, The
Galley, The
Golden Grill
Grand Hotel
Harbor Haus
House of Ludington
Keweenaw Mountain
   Lodge
Mariner North, The
Mr. B's
Nelson's
Northwoods, The
Old Country Haus
Onigaming Supper Club
Romagnoli's
Stables, The
Vierling Saloon

Ontario

Bavarian Inn Ratskeller
Blue Danube
Bridges
Brigantino
Bubi's Awesome Eats
Cajun Quarter, The

Caterings Cafe
Charly's Tavern
Chez Vins
Cook's Shop
Da Luciano
Desmond's
Ducks on the Roof
Gyliane
Harvey Lo's
Himalaya
J.B.'s Bar & Grill
J.B.'s Harbor House
Kashmir
La Cuisine
La Notte
Louie Linguini's
Lucky Kitchen

Mason-Girardot
Mini, The
Olde Country Steak
    House
Park Terrace
Plunkett's
Shin Shin
Snooty Rooster, The
Szechuan Garden
Traiteurs
Trevi
Tunnel Bar-B-Q
Ups n' Downs
Wah Court
Wong's Eatery
Wooden Spoon, The

TYPE OF CUISINE

American Traditional

Arboretum
Betty Ross II
Blaney Inn
Botsford Inn
Bower's Harbor Inn
Bridges
Chesaning Heritage
  House
Cooper's Arms
Country Jim's
Cousin Jenny's
Dam Site Inn
Dearborn Tavern
Dill's Olde Town
Dogpatch, The
E.G. Nick's
Elizabeth Street Cafe
Elizabeth's by the Lake
Embers, The
Evergreen Grill
Farm House, The
Frankenmuth Corner
  Tavern
Golden Grill, The
Grand Hotel
Grande Mare Inn
Haab's
Hathaway House
Home Sweet Home
Hotel Doherty
Iva's
Judy's Cafe
Juilleret's
Kate's Kitchen
Le Peep
Machus Sly Fox
Mayflower Hotel
Normandie
Northwoods, The
One 23
Original Pancake House
Parkside Dining Room
Pinkey's
Sindbad's
St. Clair Inn
Star of Detroit
Victorian Inn
Vierling Saloon
Whistle Stop
Zehnder's

American Contemporary

Andante
Appe'teaser II

Archers
Arie's Cafe
Beverly Hills Grill
Bouquets
Cafe Bon Homme
Cafe Jardin
Cafe Le Chat
Charley's Crab
Chez Raphael
Clarkston Cafe
Country Epicure
Cousins Heritage Inn
Cygnus
D.J. Kelly's
Danny's
Dearborn Inn
Diana's Delight
Double Eagle
Dusty's
Elaine's
Elwood
Evergreen Grill
Fairfield's
Fox & Hounds
Great Lakes Inn
Hattie's
Hillside
Historic Holly Hotel
Homestead, The
Hotel St. Regis
Ivy's in the Park
Jacques Demers
Justine
Kelly's Road House
La Becasse
La Rotisserie
Leelanau Country Inn
Les Auteurs
Little River Cafe
London Chop House
Long Branch
Lord Fox
Lorien
Macardy's
Mackinnon's
Mackinnon's Macomb Inn
Mary Ann's Kitchen
Medallion
Meritage, The
Michael's
Midtown Cafe
Miller's
Money Tree
Montague Inn
Nicky's
1913 Room, The
Oakley's
Paint Creek
Park Place Cafe

Pike Street
Prickly Pear, The
Rattlesnake Club
Richard & Reiss
Ritz-Carlton
River Bistro
Riverside Inn
Rowe Inn
Sandpiper, The
Schuler's
Sebastian's
Silky Sullivan's
Spencer Creek
Stafford's Bay View Inn
Stafford's One Water St.
Stafford's Pier
Tabor Hill
Tapawingo
Terrace Inn
Thorn Apple Village
333 East
Trillium
Van Dyke Place
Victors'
Walloon Lake Inn
Washington Street
Waterworks
Whitney, The
Windows

Argentinian

El Gaucho

Barbecue

Brothers Bar-b-que
Ginopolis'
Houlihan's
Kelly's Road House
Mitch's Tavern
Peabody's
Tunnel Bar-B-Q

Belgian

Cadieux Cafe

British

Ritz-Carlton
Snooty Rooster, The
Sweet Afton Tea Room
Ups n' Downs

Cafeteria

Britts'
Epicurean Cafe
Quattro Punti

Schnelli Deli
Steve's Soul Food
Sweet Lorraine's
   (Madison Heights)

Cajun/Creole

Cajun Quarter, The
French Market Cafe
Houlihan's
Louisiana Creole
   Gumbo
Magnolia Grille

Canadian

Chez Vins
Gyliane
Park Terrace
Tunnel Bar-B-Q
Wooden Spoon, The

Chinese

Ah Wok
Harvey Lo's
Lim's Garden
Lucky Kitchen
Mon Jin Lau
Panda, The
Peking House
Rikshaw Inn
Shin Shin
Sze-Chuan Restaurant
Szechuan Garden
Wah Court
West East Ethnic
Wing Hong
Wong's Eatery

Continental

Archers
Benno's
Bijou
Chez Raphael
Ducks on the Roof
Excalibur
Golden Mushroom
Hermann's
Hotel St. Regis
House of Ludington
Jim's Tiffany Place
Kingsley Inn
Lark, The
Little Harry's
Machus Red Fox
Mason-Girardot
Palace Grille, The
Panache

124

Rugby Grille
St. Clair Inn
Victorian Inn

Delis

Bread Basket Deli
Caterings Cafe
Deli Unique
Epicurean Cafe
Hershel's Deli
Left Field Deli
Loaf & Mug
Mary Ann's Kitchen
McNally's
Pickle Barrel
Sara's
Schnelli Deli
Stage & Co.
Star Deli
Uncle Harry's
Zingerman's
Zukin's

Dim Sum

Lucky Kitchen
Wah Court
Wong's Eatery

Ethiopian

Blue Nile, The

French

Benno's
Bijou
Cousins Heritage Inn
Cuisine de Pays
Desmond's
Earle, The
Escoffier
Golden Mushroom
Gyliane
Justine
Kerrytown Bistro
La Becasse
La Cuisine
La Rotisserie
Le Metro
Money Tree
Moveable Feast, The
Opus One
Pontchartrain Wine
   Cellars
Punchinello's
Van Dyke Place

German

Bavarian Inn
Bavarian Inn Ratskeller
Dakota Inn
Franconian, The
Glen Lake Inn
Harbor Haus
Hermann's
Jacoby's
Old Country Haus
Old German

Greek

Grecian Gardens
Jim's Tiffany Place
Laikon Cafe
Lindos Taverna
New Hellas
Niki's Pizzeria
Old Parthenon
Pegasus at the Fisher
Pegasus Taverna
Sugar Bowl

Hamburger

Anchor Bar
Andrew's
Antler's
Beau Jack's
Beggar's Banquet
Bubi's Awesome Eats
Buhl Cafe
Clementine's
Danny's
Dearborn Tavern
Del Rio
Dunleavy'z
Eddie's Drive-In
Finney's Pub
Fischer's
Galligan's
Golden Galleon
Houlihan's
Jacoby's
Kelly's Road House
Lindell A.C.
Long Branch
Metro Musicafe
Murdock's
Norman's Eton St.
Olde Town Cafe
Peanut Barrel, The
Plunkett's
Sindbad's
Sleder's
Soup Kitchen
Ted's

Traffic Jam
Tug's
Union Street
Vivio's
Wagon Wheel Saloon
Woodbridge Tavern

Hungarian

Al's Lounge
Blue Danube

Indian

Govinda's
Himalaya
Kashmir
Natraj
Passage to India
Peacock, The
Raja Rani
Sitar
Star of India

Irish

Houlihan's
O'Sullivan's

Italian

Andiamo
Antonio's
Bella Ciao
Blue Pointe
Bravo!
Brigantino
Buddy's Pizza
Cafe Cortina
Cafe Piccirilli
Carlucci
Charley's Seafood
    Taverns
Cloverleaf
Confetti's
Cook's Shop
Crispigna's
Cucina Di Pasta
Da Edoardo
Da Luciano
DePalma's
Desmond's
Earle, The
Genitti's
Giovanni's
Giulio & Sons
Gratzi
Italian Cucina
Joe Bologna
Joey's

La Notte
Lelli's
Lepanto
Louie Linguini's
Marco's
Maria's Pizzeria
Mario's
Moro's
Oliverio's
Paparazzi
Peppina's
Picano's
Pietro's
Pistachio's
Pizza Papalis
Punchinello's
R.I.K.'s
Ristorante di Maria
Ristorante di Modesta
Ristorante la Pasta
Roma Cafe
Romagnoli's
Salvatore Scallopini
Shield's
Stables, The
Tosi's
Trevi
Valente's
Vannelli Gus'
Vince's

Japanese

Akasaka
Miki
Musashi
Nipponkai
Tokyo Sushi-Iwa
Wing Hong

Mexican

Billie's Boathouse
Cafe Rio
Don Carlos
El Gaucho
El Zocalo
Finney's Pub
La Familia
La Fuente
Las Brisas
Mexican Fiesta
Mexican Town
Mexican Village
Muchachos
Xochimilco

Middle Eastern

Byblos
Gnome, The

La Shish
Murdock's
Phoenicia
Sahara
Steve's Back Room
Sultan's
Summerland
Village Cafe

Pizza

Alibi Lounge
America's Pizza Cafe
Bravo!
Buddy's Pizza
Cloverleaf
Da Edoardo (trattoria)
E.G. Nick's
Joe Bologna
Kruse & Muer
Maria's Pizzeria
Mitch's Tavern
Niki's Pizzeria
Peppina's
Pietro's
Pizza Papalis
Pizzeria Uno's
Shield's
Thorn Apple Village
  (Tap Room)
Trevi
Vince's
Wagon Wheel Saloon

Polish

Amadeus Cafe
Busia's
Ivanhoe Cafe
Legs Inn
Polish Village Cafe
Polonia
Under the Eagle

Seafood

Blaney Inn
Blue Pointe
Bluebird
Brewery, The
Bridges
Cafe du Voyageur
Charley's Crab
Charley's Seafood
  Taverns
Chicago Road House
Clamdigger's
Cooper's Arms
D. Dennison's

Excalibur
Galley, The
Gandy Dancer
Ginopolis'
Grande Mere Inn
Great Lakes Whitefish
Haab's
Harbor Haus
Hotel Doherty
Ivanhoe Cafe
J.B.'s Harbor House
Joe Muer's
Kruse & Muer
Leelanau Country Inn
Mariner North, The
Norm's Oyster Bar
Patrick's Shalea Inn
Pistachio's
Rachelle's
Real Seafood Co., The
River Bistro
River Crab
Rupperts'
Scallops
Sebastian's
Sindbad's
St. Clair Inn
Stafford's Pier
Ted's
Terry's Place
Terry's Terrace
Tidewater Grill
Tom's Oyster Bar
Tug's
Vannelli Gus'

Soul Food

Black Pearl
Steve's Soul Food

Spanish

Bagley Cafe

Steaks & Chops

Boone's
Brewery, The
Carl's Chop House
Chesaning Heritage
  House
Chicago Road House
Clementine's Too
Cooper's Arms
Dill's Olde Town
Embers, The
Excalibur
Fox & Hounds

Haab's
Hathaway House
Hotel Doherty
J.B.'s Harbor House
Keweenaw Mountain
  Lodge
Lelli's
London Chop House
Long Branch
Mario's
Mr. Paul's
Nelson's
1940 Chop House
Normandie
Olde Country Steak
  House
Onigaming Supper Club
Oxford Inn
Peabody's
Portside Inn
Schuler's
Shannon's
Silky Sullivan's
Sindbad's
St. Clair Inn
Summit, The
Sweet Water Wharf
Ted's
Treasure Island
Vannelli Gus'

Teas

Cafe Le Chat
Monchelle Lamoure
Ritz-Carlton
Rugby Grille
Snooty Rooster, The
Sweet Afton Tea Room

Thai

Bangkok Club
Bangkok Cuisine
Bangkok Express
Siam Spicy
Thai Classic Cuisine
Thai House
Thai Inn
West East Ethnic

Turkish

Mason-Girardot

Upscale

Andante
Archers

Bouquets
Cafe Bon Homme
Cafe Cortina
Cafe Le Chat
Cafe Piccirilli
Charley's Crab
Chez Raphael
Cousins Heritage Inn
Cygnus
Da Edoardo
Elaine's
Escoffier
Golden Mushroom
Hattie's
Justine
La Becasse
La Rotisserie
Lark, The
London Chop House
Money Tree
Oakley's
Opus One
Palace Grille, The
Park Terrace
Pike Street
Rattlesnake Club
Ritz-Carlton
Rowe Inn
Sandpiper, The
Spencer Creek
Tapawingo
Trillium
Van Dyke Place
Victors'
Walloon Lake Inn
Whitney, The
Windows

Vegetarian

Bangkok Club
Bangkok Cuisine
Bangkok Express
Britts'
Byblos
Caterings Cafe
Del Rio
Gnome, The
Govinda's
Grain Train
Himalaya
Inn Season
Kashmir
Natraj
Om Cafe
Passage to India
Peacock, The
Phoenicia
Pure n' Simple
Raja Rani
Sahara
Seva

128

Siam Spicy
Sitar
Soho Cafe
Star of India
Steve's Back Room
Sultan's
Summerland
Thai Classic Cuisine
Thai House
Thai Inn
Traffic Jam

Village Cafe
West East Ethnic

Vietnamese

Mini, The
West East Ethnic

SPECIAL FEATURES

Five Stars

Chez Raphael
Golden Mushroom
Lark, The
Zingerman's

Four Stars

Beverly Hills Grill
Bread Basket Deli
Cafe Le Chat
Clarkston Cafe
Cousins Heritage Inn
Cuisine de Pays
Cygnus
Da Edoardo
Escoffier
Hattie's
Justine
Kruse & Muer
La Becasse
La Rotisserie
Le Metro
Les Auteurs
London Chop House
Lorien
Money Tree
1913 Room, The
Oliverio's
Opus One
Pike Street
R.I.K.'s
Rattlesnake Club
Ritz-Carlton
Rowe Inn
Sandpiper, The
Sweet Afton Tea Room
Tapawingo
Traffic Jam
Van Dyke Place
Whitney, The
Windows

After-Theatre

Alexander's
Elwood
Finney's Pub
Gnome, The
Lelli's
Les Auteurs
London Chop House
Mario's
1940 Chop House
Normandie
O'Sullivan's

On Stage
Opus One
Pegasus at the Fisher
Rattlesnake Club
Roma Cafe
Traffic Jam
Union Street
Whitney, The

Bargain

Al's Lounge
Alibi Lounge
Amadeus Cafe
American/Lafayette
    Coney Island
Andrew's
Arie's Cafe
Bagley Cafe
Bangkok Cuisine
Bangkok Express
Betty Ross II
Black Pearl
Blue Pointe
Boone's
Bubi's Awesome Eats
Busia's
Caterings Cafe
Clementine's
Clementine's Too
Country Jim's
Cuisine de Pays
Da Edoardo (trattoria)
Deli Unique
Eddie's Drive-In
Elizabeth Street Cafe
Epicurean Cafe
Fischer's
Frankenmuth Corner
    Tavern
French Market Cafe
Genitti's
Golden Grill
Great Lakes Whitefish
Haab's
Home Sweet Home
Joe Bologna
Judy's Cafe
Kashmir
La Fuente
Mexican Fiesta
Mexican Town
Mexican Village
Mr. B's
Picano's
Polish Village
Polonia
Salvatore Scallopini

Sara's
Schnelli Deli
Star Deli
Steve's Soul Food
Summerland
Terry's Terrace
West East Ethnic

Bar Scene

Anchor Bar
Andrew's
Antler's
Archers
Brewery, The
Carl's Chop House
Charly's Tavern
Country Epicure
Danny's
Dunleavy'z
Elwood
Excalibur
Fox & Hounds
Golden Galleon
Houlihan's
Jacques Demers
Kelly's Road House
Kerrytown Bistro
Kingsley Inn
Lansdowne
Lindell A.C.
Little Harry's
London Chop House
Meritage, The
Midtown Cafe
Money Tree
Murdock's
Nicky's
Norman's Eton St.
One 23
Opus One
Palace Grille, The
Panache
Peabody's
Pegasus at the Fisher
Rattlesnake Club
Ristorante di Modesta
Rugby Grille
Sindbad's
Sparky Herberts
220 Merrill St.
Woodbridge Tavern

Beautiful

Cafe Bon Homme
Cafe Cortina
Cafe Le Chat
Charley's Crab
Chez Raphael
Cygnus

Dearborn Inn
Gandy Dancer
Govinda's
Homestead, The
Lark, The
Mason-Girardot
Meritage, The
1913 Room, The
Opus One
Ritz-Carlton
Stafford's Bay View
Sweet Afton Tea Room
Van Dyke Place
Victorian Inn
Whitney, The

Beer Lists of Note

Cadieux Cafe
Charly's Tavern
Dusty's
Galligan's
Legs Inn
Murdock's
O'Sullivan's
Old German
Plunkett's
Seva
Soup Kitchen
Sweet Lorraine's
Tom's Oyster Bar
Traffic Jam
Traiteurs
Union Street

Best Values

Angelo's
Bangkok Cuisine
Beverly Hills Grill
Bread Basket Deli
Britts'
Cousin Jenny's
Cuisine de Pays
Judy's Cafe
Kruse & Muer
Lorien
Quattro Punti
Seva
Soho Cafe
Sweet Afton Tea Room
Traffic Jam
Zingerman's

Breakfast

Angelo's
Beggar's Banquet

Betty Ross II
Beverly Hills Grill
Botsford Inn
Bridges
Britts'
Busia's
Caterings Cafe
Country Jim's
Dearborn Inn
Diana's Delight
Dogpatch, The
Elizabeth Street Cafe
Epicurean Cafe
Frankenmuth Corner
    Tavern
Golden Grill
Hershel's Deli
Hotel Doherty
Juilleret's
Kate's Kitchen
Kingsley Inn
Le Peep
Left Field Deli
Mary Ann's Kitchen
Mayflower Hotel
Moveable Feast, The
Mr. B's
O'Sullivan's
Original Pancake House
Parkside Dining Room
Quattro Punti
Richard & Reiss
Riverside Inn
Stafford's Bay View
Sugar Bowl
Terry's Terrace
Tunnel Bar-B-Q
Vierling Saloon
Vivio's
Whistle Stop
Wooden Spoon
Zingerman's

Lelli's
Les Auteurs
London Chop House
Macardy's
Machus Red Fox
Machus Sly Fox
Meritage, The
Michael's
Midtown Cafe
Mon Jin Lau
Money Tree
Mr. Paul's
Musashi
1913 Room, The
1940 Chop House
One 23
Opus One
Park Terrace
Phoenicia
Pike Street
Pontchartrain Wine
    Cellars
Punchinello's
Rattlesnake Club
Ristorante di Modesta
Ritz-Carlton
River Bistro
Roma Cafe
Rugby Grille
Sebastian's
Shannon's
Silky Sullivan's
Sindbad's
Soup Kitchen
333 East
Traffic Jam
220 Merrill St.
Victors'
Village Cafe
Wagon Wheel Saloon
Washington Street
West East Ethnic
Whitney, The
Wong's Eatery

Business Lunches

Archers
Bangkok Club
Bangkok Cuisine
Bijou
Carl's Chop House
Charley's Crab
Excalibur
Fairfield's
Fox & Hounds
Ginopolis'
Golden Mushroom
Hotel St. Regis
Ivy's in the Park
Jacoby's
Joe Muer's
Kingsley Inn
La Familia

Carryout

Bread Basket Deli
Buddy's Pizza
Caterings Cafe
Cousin Jenny's
Cucina Di Pasta
Deli Unique
E.G. Nick's
Elizabeth Street Cafe
Epicurean Cafe
Grain Train
Hershel's Deli
Inn Season
Joe Bologna
Kruse & Muer
Left Field Deli

Les Auteurs
Lim's Garden
Loaf & Mug
Louisiana Creole
   Gumbo
Lucky Kitchen
Mary Ann's Kitchen
McNally's
Peking House
Pickle Barrel
Pizzeria Uno's
Prickly Pear, The
R.I.K.'s
Richard & Reiss
Riverside Inn
Sara's
Schnelli Deli
Star Deli
Steve's Back Room
Sweet Lorraine's
Thai Inn
Uncle Harry's
Zingerman's
Zukin's

Critic's Choice

Bagley Cafe
Beverly Hills Grill
Britts'
Da Edoardo
Golden Mushroom
Kruse & Muer
London Chop House
Lorien
Money Tree
Pike Street
Rattlesnake Club
Roma Cafe
Rowe Inn
Sultan's
Traffic Jam
Whitney, The

Dancing

Cygnus
Excalibur
Fox & Hounds
J. B.'s Bar & Grill
Joey's
La Rotisserie
London Chop House
Metro Musicafe
Nicky's
Panache
Ritz-Carlton
Sebastian's
Sweet Water Wharf
Wooly Bully's

Desserts

Bubi's Awesome Eats
Charley's Crab
Country Epicure
Cousins Heritage Inn
Deli Unique
Farm House, The
Hermann's
Hershel's Deli
Italian Cucina
Joe Bologna
Juilleret's
Kate's Kitchen
Lorien
Machus Red Fox
Machus Sly Fox
Monchelle Lamoure
Money Tree
Moveable Feast, The
On Stage
Opus One
Rattlesnake Club
Seva
Susan Hoffmann
Sweet Lorraine's
Traffic Jam
Traiteurs
Tunnel Bar-B-Q
Whistle Stop
Whitney, The
Windows

Eclectic

Alban's
Beggar's Banquet
Bubi's Awesome Eats
Caterings Cafe
Chez Vins
Del Rio
Dusty's
Earle, The
Galligan's
Inn Season
Kerrytown Bistro
Les Auteurs
Maude's
Moro's
Mr. B's
On Stage
Potpourri
R.P. McMurphy's
Rachelle's
Rhinoceros, The
Soho
Sparky Herberts
Susan Hoffmann
Sweet Lorraine's
Traffic Jam
Traiteurs
220 Merrill St.

Union Street
Washington Street

Entertainment

Alexander's
Billie's Boathouse
Blue Danube
Cafe Bon Homme
Cafe Piccirilli
Caucus Club
Cuisine de Pays
Cygnus
Dakota Inn
Danny's
Double Eagle
Excalibur
Fox & Hounds
Gnome, The
Historic Holly Hotel
La Rotisserie
Las Brisas
Legs Inn
Little Harry's
London Chop House
Long Branch
Metro Musicafe
Mr. Paul's
Murdock's
Nicky's
1940 Chop House
Panache
Picano's
Pinkey's
Prickly Pear, The
Rattlesnake Club
Rhinoceros, The
Sebastian's
Soup Kitchen
Sweet Water Wharf
Whitney, The
Woodbridge Tavern
Wooly Bully's

Health-Conscious

Beau Jack's
Blue Nile, The
Britts'
Bubi's Awesome Eats
Caterings Cafe
Confetti's
Cooper's Arms
Cucina Di Pasta
Evergreen Grill
Golden Mushroom
Govinda's
Grain Train
Hermann's
Himalaya
Hogan's

Houlihan's
Inn Season
Loaf & Mug
Magnolia Grille
Mini, The
Om Cafe
Pure n' Simple
Richard & Reiss
Seva
Soho
Sweet Lorraine's
Traffic Jam
West East Ethnic

Hidden Gems

Angelo's
Bagley Cafe
Bangkok Cuisine
Bella Ciao
Blue Nile, The
Bread Basket Deli
Brigantino
Cafe Le Chat
Cook's Shop
Kashmir
Kruse & Muer
Lorien
Siam Spicy
Steve's Back Room
Whistle Stop

Kitchen
Open Late

American/Lafayette
    Coney Island
Hershel's Deli
Lim's Garden
London Chop House
Long Branch
Midtown Cafe
1940 Chop House
Peabody's
Roma Cafe
Stage & Co.
Traiteurs
Village Cafe

Lunch Hot Spots

Appe'teaser II
Bangkok Cuisine
Betty Ross II
Bijou
Britts'
Buhl Cafe
Cafe Jardin
Cafe Rio

Carl's Chop House
Caterings Cafe
Caucus Club
Charley's Crab
Country Epicure
Diana's Delight
Elizabeth Street Cafe
Elizabeth's by the Lake
Epicurean Cafe
Fairfield's
Genitti's
Golden Mushroom
Govinda's
Gyliane
Houlihan's
Inn Season
Ivanhoe Cafe
Jacoby's
Jim's Tiffany Place
Kate's Kitchen
La Palette
Le Peep
Left Field Deli
Lorien
Lucky Kitchen
Machus Sly Fox
Maude's
Michael's
Monchelle Lamoure
Money Tree
Natraj
Normandie
Old German
One 23
Parkside Dining Room
Peacock, The
Pontchartrain Wine
  Cellars
Quattro Punti
Rattlesnake Club
Richard & Reiss
Snooty Rooster, The
Sweet Afton Tea Room
Thai Inn
Traffic Jam
Village Cafe
Wah Court
Whistle Stop

Newly Opened

America's Pizza Cafe
Andante
Andiamo
Bangkok Club
Le Metro
Mackinnon's Macomb
  Inn
Marco's
Meritage, The
O'Sullivan's
Paparazzi

Ristorante la Pasta
Thai House

Offbeat

Antler's, The
Bubi's Awesome Eats
Clamdigger's
Clementine's
Eddie's Drive-in
Elwood
Home Sweet Home
Kola's Kitchen
Left Field Deli
Legs Inn
Wooly Bully's

Out With the Gang

Al's Lounge
Antler's, The
Brothers Bar-b-que
Bubi's Awesome Eats
Buddy's Pizza
Cadieux Cafe
Carl's Chop House
Charly's Tavern
Clementine's
Cloverleaf
Dakota Inn
Dill's Olde Town
Dogpatch, The
Dunleavy'z
E.G. Nick's
Finney's Pub
Fischer's
Galligan's
Great Lakes Whitefish
Hathaway House
Houlihan's
Jacoby's
Kelly's Road House
La Familia
Las Brisas
Legs Inn
Lindell A.C.
Mexican Fiesta
Niki's Pizzeria
O'Sullivan's
Old German
Peabody's
Peanut Barrel, The
Peppina's
Pizzeria Uno's
Plunkett's
Sindbad's
Soup Kitchen
Terry's Terrace
Traffic Jam
Wagon Wheel Saloon
Woodbridge Tavern

Wooly Bully's
Xochimilco

Outdoor Dining

Andrew's
Carlucci
Country Epicure
Danny's
Elwood
Galligan's
Gandy Dancer
Gratzi
Les Auteurs
Midtown Cafe
Money Tree
Niki's Pizzeria
Portside Inn
Rattlesnake Club
River Crab
Soup Kitchen
Woodbridge Tavern

Convenient to Palace/Silverdome

Clarkston Cafe
Kruse & Muer
La Familia
Long Branch
Palace Grille, The
Patrick's Shalea Inn
Pike Street
Vannelli Gus'

Peaceful Setting

Akasaka
Antonio's
Bagley Cafe
Benno's
Byblos
Cafe Cortina
Cafe Le Chat
Chez Raphael
Chez Vins
Clarkston Cafe
Da Edoardo
Escoffier
Govinda's
Hattie's
Himalaya
Historic Holly Hotel
Homestead, The
Justine's
La Palette
Lark, The
Legs Inn
Miki

Moveable Feast, The
Natraj
Oxford Inn
Passage to India
Potpourri Cafe
Sahara
Spencer Creek
Stafford's One Water St.
Stafford's Pier
Sultan's
Sweet Afton Tea Room
Van Dyke Place
Victorian Inn
Walloon Lake Inn

People-Watching

Andante
Caucus Club
Confetti's
Elwood
Excalibur
Ginopolis'
Golden Mushroom
Jacques Demers
Kingsley Inn
Les Auteurs
Lindell A.C.
London Chop House
Machus Red Fox
Midtown Cafe
Mon Jin Lau
Money Tree
1940 Chop House
Oliverio's
Phoenicia
R.I.K.'s
Rattlesnake Club
Ristorante di Modesta
Rugby Grille
Sindbad's
Sparky Herberts
Stafford's Pier
Tom's Oyster Bar

Power Scene

Archers
Bijou
Carl's Chop House
Caucus Club
Chez Raphael
Excalibur
Fairfield's
Fox & Hounds
Golden Mushroom
Hotel St. Regis
Jim's Tiffany Place
Joe Muer's
Lark, The
Lelli's

Les Auteurs
London Chop House
Machus Red Fox
Meritage, The
Midtown Cafe
Mon Jin Lau
Money Tree
Mr. Paul's
Nicky's
1940 Chop House
Normandie
Opus One
Pontchartrain Wine
  Cellars
Rattlesnake Club
Ristorante di Modesta
Roma Cafe
Silky Sullivan's
Stafford's One Water St.
Whitney, The

Private Rooms

Akasaka
Carl's Chop House
Country Epicure
Fox & Hounds
Ginopolis'
Italian Cucina
Joe Muer's
Kingsley Inn
Les Auteurs
Lord Fox
Machus Red Fox
Meritage, The
Nipponkai
Pinkey's
Pontchartrain Wine
  Cellars
Rattlesnake Club
Ritz-Carlton
Rugby Grille
Thai Classic Cuisine
Tokyo Sushi-Iwa
Traffic Jam
Van Dyke Place
Whitney, The
Xochimilco

Romantic

Andante
Andiamo
Antonio's
Bagley Cafe
Bella Ciao
Benno's
Blue Nile, The
Cafe Bon Homme
Cafe Cortina
Cafe Le Chat

Cajun Quarter
Caucus Club
Charley's Crab
Chez Raphael
Chez Vins
Confetti's
Cook's Shop
Cousins Heritage Inn
Cuisine de Pays
Cygnus
Da Edoardo
Da Luciano
Dearborn Inn
Double Eagle
Ducks on the Roof
Earle, The
Escoffier
Golden Mushroom
Gyliane
Hattie's
La Rotisserie
Lark, The
Lepanto
Louie Linguini's
Mason-Girardot
Medallion
Monchelle Lamoure
Moveable Feast, The
1913 Room, The
Opus One
Passage to India
Raja Rani
Rugby Grille
Spencer Creek
Valente's
Van Dyke Place
Walloon Lake Inn

Room With a View

Andante
Bluebird
Carlucci
Cygnus
Double Eagle
Homestead, The
Legs Inn
Park Terrace
Portside Inn
Prickly Pear, The
Sandpiper, The
St. Clair Inn
Stafford's One Water St.
Star of Detroit
Summit, The
Tabor Hill
Thorn Apple Village
Trillium
Vierling Saloon
Windows

Singles

Andrew's
Danny's
Finney's Pub
Galligan's
Houlihan's
Joey's
Metro Musicafe
Midtown Cafe
Norman's Eton St.
Panache
Rhinoceros, The
Soup Kitchen
Sparky Herberts
220 Merrill St.
Union Street
Wagon Wheel Saloon
Woodbridge Tavern
Wooly Bully's

Sunday Brunch

Amadeus Cafe
Beggar's Banquet
Beverly Hills Grill
Blue Pointe
Botsford Inn
Bower's Harbor Inn
Bravo!
Bridges Restaurant
Carlucci
Charley's Crab
Cloverleaf
Dearborn Inn
Deli Unique
Desmond's
Dogpatch, The
Double Eagle
Dusty's
Elaine's
Elizabeth's by the Lake
Embers, The
Evergreen Grill
Fairfield's
Franconian, The
French Market Cafe
Gandy Dancer
Giulio & Sons
Gnome, The
Hillside
Hotel Doherty
Hotel St. Regis
Houlihan's
House of Ludington
Ivy's in the Park
J.B.'s Harbor House
Jacques Demers
Jim's Tiffany Place
Kerrytown Bistro

Keweenaw Mountain Lodge
Lansdowne
Le Peep
Leelanau Country Inn
Loaf & Mug
Machus Sly Fox
Mayflower Hotel
Meritage, The
Michael's
Midtown Cafe
1913 Room, The
Norman's Eton St.
Northwoods, The
Olde Country Steak House
Paint Creek
Park Terrace
Pistachio's
Polonia
Rachelle's
Rhinoceros, The
Ritz-Carlton
River Crab
Schuler's
Seva
Sparky Herberts
Stafford's Bay View
Star of Detroit
Summit, The
Tabor Hill
Trillium
Washington Street
Whitney, The
Woodbridge Tavern

Sunday Night

Alban's
Antonio's
Blue Nile, The
Cafe Cortina
Carl's Chop House
Charley's Seafood Taverns
Cloverleaf
Confetti's
Cook's Shop
Double Eagle
Ducks on the Roof
Elizabeth's by the Lake
Grecian Gardens
Hershel's Deli
Home Sweet Home
Hotel Doherty
Houlihan's
Jacques Demers
Laikon Cafe
Lindos Taverna
Lucky Kitchen
Midtown Cafe
Mitch's Tavern

Mon Jin Lau
Murdock's
Musashi
Natraj
New Hellas
Niki's Pizza
1940 Chop House
Old Parthenon
Oliverio's
Peacock, The
Pegasus Taverna
Picano's
Punchinello's
Pure n' Simple
Ristorante di Maria
Rhinoceros, The
Ritz-Carlton (Grill Room)
Rugby Grille
Sindbad's
Stage & Co.
Star of India
Terry's Terrace
Traiteurs
Valente's
Village Cafe
Wagon Wheel Saloon
Whitney, The

Take the Kids

Alban's
Alibi Lounge
Arie's Cafe
Bavarian Inn
Betty Ross II
Billie's Boathouse
Blue Pointe
Bread Basket Deli
Bubi's Awesome Eats
Buddy's Pizza
Busia's
Cadieux Cafe
Charley's Seafood
  Taverns
Clementine's
Clementine's Too
Cloverleaf
Country Jim's
Cousin Jenny's
D. Dennison's
Dam Site Inn
Deli Unique
DePalma's
Dogpatch, The
Don Carlos
E.G. Nick's
Eddie's Drive-in
El Gaucho
El Zocalo
Fischer's
Frankenmuth Corner
  Tavern

Galley, The
Ginopolis'
Golden Grill
Great Lakes Whitefish
Haab's
Hillside
Hogan's
Home Sweet Home
Houlihan's
Iva's
Joe Bologna
Juilleret's
Kelly's Road House
Keweenau Mountain
  Lodge
La Familia
La Fuente
Las Brisas
Legs Inn
Lim's Garden
Loaf & Mug
Macardy's
Marco's
Mexican Fiesta
Mexican Town
Mexican Village
Mitch's Tavern
Mr. B's
Muchachos
Old Parthenon
Original Pancake House
Parkside Dining Room
Peabody's
Peking House
Peppina's
Pizzeria Uno's
Polish Village
Polonia
Salvatore Scallopini
Sara's
Shield's
Stafford's Bay View
Stage & Co.
Terry's Terrace
Tidewater Grill
Trevi
Tunnel Bar-B-Q
Zehnder's

Top Tables

Chez Raphael: #22
Golden Mushroom: #1
Lark, The: #9
Les Auteurs: #52
London Chop House:
  Booth 1
Opus One: #9
Rattlesnake Club: #12
Ritz-Carlton (The
  Restaurant): #53

Van Dyke Place: #6
Whitney, The: #36

Wine Lists of Note

Alban's
Arboretum
Beggar's Banquet
Bijou
Chez Raphael
Chez Vins
Cuisine de Pays
Da Edoardo
Dusty's
Earle, The
Escoffier
Fox & Hounds
Giovanni's
Golden Mushroom
Kerrytown Bistro
Lark, The
Little River Cafe
London Chop House
Lord Fox
Mackinnon's
Michael's
Money Tree
New Hellas
1940 Chop House
Oakley's
Opus One
Pike Street
Rattlesnake Club
Rowe Inn
Sparky Herberts
Tapawingo
Tosi's
Traffic Jam
Van Dyke Place
Whitney, The

SPECIAL LISTINGS

GOURMET-TO-GO & CATERERS
(in Metro Detroit area)

Back Alley Gourmet, The
South Main Market, 111 E. Mosley, Ann
Arbor, 662–1175.

Baker's Loaf
29480 Northwestern Hwy., Southfield,
354–5623.

Gourmet House
25225 E. Jefferson, St. Clair Shores, 771–0300.
Catering only. No retail.

Great Scott!
Call 943–3300 for store locations of gourmet
carryouts.

Hugo's Gourmet Deli
19795 Mack, Grosse Point Woods, 886–6060.

Juliette's Cuisine/division of Merchant of Vino
Locations: 254 W. Maple, Birmingham,
433–3000; 29525 Northwestern Hwy.,
Southfield, 354–6505; 4050 Rochester Rd.,
Troy, 689–0900.

L.A. Express at Les Auteurs
222 Sherman Dr., Royal Oak, 544–2372.

Mark of Excellence
26211 Central Park Blvd., Suite 319,
Southfield, 352–5863. Catering only. No retail.

Moveable Feast
407 N. Fifth, Kerrytown, 663–3331.

Pasta Deli Pasta
31109 Greenfield, Birmingham, 258–9797.

Peter's Palate Pleaser Inc.
1087 W. Long Lake, Bloomfield Hills,
540–2266.

Pizza Gourmet
P.O. Box 90, Plymouth, 451-0005.
Off-premises catering only. No retail.

Queen of Cups Catering Consultants
Grosse Pointe, 884-0620. Specialty production
catering only. No retail.

R.I.K.'s Total Cuisine Center
6646 Telegraph, Birmingham, 855-4005. Also
R.I.K.'s Carryout adjacent to R.I.K.'s the
Restaurant, Orchard Mall, 6303 Orchard Lake
Rd., West Bloomfield, 855-9889.

Sarah's
8027 Agnes, Detroit, 824-6666.

Savory Fare Ltd.
(in Cheese & Wine Barn), 515 Forest,
Plymouth, 454-9669.

Zingerman's Delicatessen
422 Detroit, Ann Arbor, 663-3354.

PREMIUM WINE SHOPS
(in Metro Detroit area)

Beverage Warehouse,
31111 Greenfield (n. of 13 Mile), Birmingham,
644-2155.

Big Ten Party Store,
1428 Packard (s. of Stadium Blvd.), Ann
Arbor, 662-0798.

Bottle & Basket Shoppe,
6535 Telegraph (at Maple), Birmingham,
646-6484. Also 190 N. Hunter (n. of Maple),
Birmingham, 258-5555.

Cheese & Wine Barn,
515 Forest (s. of Ann Arbor Trail), Plymouth,
453-1700.

Clover Wine Cellar,
10988 Allen Rd. (at Goddard), Taylor,
292-7642.

Cloverleaf Market, 28905 Telegraph (at 12
Mile), Southfield, 357-0400.

Cost Plus,
Eastern Market, 2448 Market, Detroit,
259-3845.

Farms Market of Grosse Pointe,
355 Fisher Rd. (bet. Jefferson and Kercheval),
Grosse Pointe, 882-5100.

Gibb's World Wide Wine,
9999 Gratiot (2 blks. n. of I-94, Gratiot exit),
Detroit, 921-6581.

Good Time Party Store,
567 Seven Mile (at Northville Rd.), Northville,
349-1477.

Merchant of Vino,
254 W. Maple (w. of Woodward),
Birmingham, 433-3000. Also 29525
Northwestern Hwy. (n. of 12 Mile), Southfield,
354-6505; 4050 Rochester Rd. (at Wattles),
Troy, 689-0900.

Partners in Wine,
111 E. Mosley (in South Main Market), Ann
Arbor, 761-2333. Also 407 N. Fifth (in
Kerrytown), Ann Arbor, 761-6384.

Red Wagon Wine Shoppe (The),
1571 N. Main (at Maple), Clawson, 435-0719.
Also 2940 Rochester Rd. (at Auburn Rd.),
Rochester, 852-9307.

Village Corner,
601 S. Forest (at S. University), Ann Arbor,
995-1818.

Village Wine Shop,
15228 E. Jefferson (at Beaconsfield), Grosse
Pointe Park, 821-1177.

Vineyards Wine Cellar (The),
32418 Northwestern Hwy. (bet. Middlebelt and
14 Mile), Farmington Hills, 855-9463.

Vintage Wine Shoppe,
41455 W. 10 Mile (in Novi Plaza), Novi,
348-3155.

Wine Castle,
33415 Seven Mile (at Farmington Rd.),
Livonia, 477-5533.

Ye Olde Wine Shoppe,
2044 W. South Blvd. (at Crooks), Rochester
Hills, 852-5533.

PERSONAL FAVORITES

Restaurant: _____

Phone #: _____

Comments: _____

_____

_____

Restaurant: _____

Phone #: _____

Comments: _____

_____

_____

Restaurant: _____

Phone #: _____

Comments: _____

_____

_____

Restaurant: _____

Phone #: _____

Comments: _____

_____

_____

Restaurant: _____

Phone #: _____

Comments: _____

_____

_____

Restaurant: _____

Phone #: _____

Comments: _____

_____

_____

PERSONAL FAVORITES

Restaurant: _____
Phone #: _____
Comments: _____
_____
_____

Restaurant: _____
Phone #: _____
Comments: _____
_____
_____

Restaurant: _____
Phone #: _____
Comments: _____
_____
_____

Restaurant: _____
Phone #: _____
Comments: _____
_____
_____

Restaurant: _____
Phone #: _____
Comments: _____
_____
_____

Restaurant: _____
Phone #: _____
Comments: _____
_____
_____

ACKNOWLEDGEMENTS

Debts are not easily paid. But without incurring them, this little volume would not have gotten past the appetizers.

Without the enthusiasm of publisher Bill Haney and assistant Natasha Monchak, I doubt this book would have made it to the main course. And without the cooperation of *The Detroit News*, there would certainly have been no chocolate mousse.

Throughout this project, there has been the encouragement of my husband, Pete, who kept prodding "go on, get it done!" and the assistance of computer-literate friends Ted Douglas, Grant Kersey, Don Reno, and Mike Achorn.

In case you wonder about the terrific Upper Peninsula entries, I have Tom BeVier of *The News* and freelance writer Dixie Franklin of Marquette to thank for their suggestions. Chef Douglas Becker of the Thomas Edison Inn in Port Huron recommended restaurants in Sarnia, Ontario. Brad Burke helped with downtown Detroit, and Sharon Stein offered useful tips on the suburbs.

To all my family, friends, and colleagues, I say thank you for exploring restaurants with me, particularly Annabel and Alex Drury, Jean and Ed Smith, Ann Sweeney, and a discreet couple known as Mr. and Mrs. Spy. Other terrific "special agents" include my friends in the wine business—everybody from wholesale to retail. To all of you, warm thanks for your contributions.

Dr. Richard Ryan and Mark Stanger gave the manuscript a critical and careful reading.

Readers of my stories in *The News*—especially those who call or write letters to make recommendations—are certainly appreciated, too. Without you, there would be no need for all this fuss about where to eat.

Above all, hugs to the restaurateurs and chefs for giving me something to write about. Nobody works harder than you do.

S.S.

NOTES

NOTES

WE WANT TO KNOW
WHAT YOU THINK

We invite you to tell us about restaurants we haven't
included here that you think merit consideration.
Give us your opinion of restaurants treated herein
which you have visited. Feel free to attach notes, if
you like.

_____

_____

_____

_____

_____

_____

_____

_____

Please put me on your mailing list for information
about the 1991 edition of POCKET GUIDE TO
DETROIT & MICHIGAN RESTAURANTS:

_____
Name

_____
Address

_____
City, State, Zip

_____
Phone Number

Return to:
Momentum Books Ltd.
2051 Warrington Road
Suite 100
Rochester Hills, MI 48063

TIP GUIDE

A 15 percent gratuity is typical when service is satisfactory, but when it surpasses expectations an increase to 18 or 20 percent should be considered, especially in upscale restaurants.

Bill	15%	20%	Bill	15%	20%
$1	.15	.20	$51	7.65	10.20
2	.30	.40	52	7.80	10.40
3	.45	.60	53	7.95	10.60
4	.60	.80	54	8.10	10.80
5	.75	1.00	55	8.25	11.00
6	.90	1.20	56	8.40	11.20
7	1.05	1.40	57	8.55	11.40
8	1.20	1.60	58	8.70	11.60
9	1.35	1.80	59	8.85	11.80
10	1.50	2.00	60	9.00	12.00
11	1.65	2.20	61	9.15	12.20
12	1.80	2.40	62	9.30	12.40
13	1.95	2.60	63	9.45	12.60
14	2.10	2.80	64	9.60	12.80
15	2.25	3.00	65	9.75	13.00
16	2.40	3.20	66	9.90	13.20
17	2.55	3.40	67	10.05	13.40
18	2.70	3.60	68	10.20	13.60
19	2.85	3.80	69	10.35	13.80
20	3.00	4.00	70	10.50	14.00
21	3.15	4.20	71	10.65	14.20
22	3.30	4.40	72	10.80	14.40
23	3.45	4.60	73	10.95	14.60
24	3.60	4.80	74	11.05	14.80
25	3.75	5.00	75	11.25	15.00
26	3.90	5.20	76	11.40	15.20
27	4.05	5.40	77	11.55	15.40
28	4.20	5.60	78	11.70	15.60
29	4.35	5.80	79	11.85	15.80
30	4.50	6.00	80	12.00	16.00
31	4.65	6.20	81	12.15	16.20
32	4.80	6.40	82	12.30	16.40
33	5.95	6.60	83	12.45	16.60
34	5.10	6.80	84	12.60	16.80
35	5.25	7.00	85	12.75	17.00
36	5.40	7.20	86	12.90	17.20
37	5.55	7.40	87	13.05	17.40
38	5.70	7.60	88	13.20	17.60
39	5.85	6.80	89	13.35	17.80
40	6.00	7.00	90	13.50	18.00
41	6.15	7.20	91	13.65	18.20
42	6.30	7.40	92	13.80	18.40
43	6.45	7.60	93	14.95	18.60
44	6.60	7.80	94	14.10	18.80
45	6.75	8.00	95	14.25	19.00
46	6.90	8.20	96	14.40	19.20
47	7.05	8.40	97	14.55	19.40
48	7.20	8.60	98	14.70	19.60
49	7.35	8.80	99	14.85	19.80
50	7.50	9.00	100	15.00	20.00